T...

BUSINESS OF

CO-PARENTING

FOR DADS

How to Establish a Parenting Partnership
&
Live Drama Free

MERISSA V. GRAYSON, ESQ.

I hope this book blesses you

1

MVG Publishing c/o Merissa V. Grayson, 21151 S. Western Ave., Torrance, CA 90501

Ordering Information:
Quantity sales. Special discounts are available on quantity purchases by corporations, associations, non-profits, and others. For details, contact the publisher at the address above.
Orders by U.S. trade bookstores and wholesalers. Please contact info@americasblendedfamilyexpert.com

Library of Congress Cataloging-in-Publication Data

Merissa V. Grayson, Esq.
The Business of Co-Parenting for Dads: How to Establish a Parenting Partnership & Live Drama Free

Edited by: Ebony Finley
Published By: MVG Publishing
Printed in the United States of America

Disclaimer: This book is intended only as an informative guide for those seeking tips for better co-parenting. This book is for informational purposes only. The suggestions and strategies contained herein may not be suitable for your situation. You should consult with a professional therapist, coach, or attorney independently where appropriate, as neither the publisher nor the author will assume responsibility for any consequences of actions taken based upon the information herein. Although the author made efforts to provide quality information, the author does not make any promises, claims, or guarantees about the adequacy, or completeness of the information. As legal advice must be specifically tailored to the facts and circumstances of each case, the legal information contained herein is for informational purposes only and does not constitute legal advice. It is neither intended to create nor does create an attorney-client relationship. Should you need legal advice, you should consult with an attorney independently.

Dedication

For my husband

Proof that with patience, perseverance, and amnesty, a cohesive divided family can exist, even after calamity.

CONTENTS

PREFACE

Today, I am a Child Custody Attorney, Mediator, and Co-Parent Coach. I've been referred to as "America's Blended Family Expert" in part because of the work that I do in helping parents learn to co-parent successfully. But, it seems like just yesterday that my family fit the profile of a reality tv show. Move over "The Real Housewives" and "Love & Hip Hop."

I am a wife to an amazing man and a mother to three children who bring so much light to my world. One of my children is technically my stepson, whom I love as if he were my biological child. I've been his bonus mom for almost eleven years now. *Now*, I'd say we fit the profile of an "ideal" blended family. But, it hasn't always been this way. We've been through it all: fights, an intense custody battle, restraining orders, jail, police intervention, sadness, anger, frustrations, confusion and eventually understanding, appreciation, happiness… and *finally* peace. You might be reading this thinking that your situation is too far gone, and I remember when my husband and I felt the same way. However, after years of trial and error, and learning some valuable lessons, our lives changed for the better and we created what feels like magic; two separate homes filled with harmony, peace and love.

Years later, when I opened my family law practice, I began to notice a recurring trend in the families I worked with. It seemed that even after my clients' legal issues were resolved, the struggle to co-parent cooperatively remained. Getting a legal "order" did nothing to change the day-to-day conflict or drama that their families faced. Their lives seemed to mirror the life I had prior to figuring out how to resolve my own co-parenting issues. So, I started working with my clients, sharing some of the strategies my family implemented and encouraging them to make a positive shift in the way they think and co-parent. As a result, many have achieved a level of peace that custody orders alone do not afford.

The Business of Co-Parenting series was inspired after looking back on my journey and realizing not only how drastically my family's life had changed for the better, but also the overwhelming positive changes in my clients' lives when we worked together to implement the same strategies that worked for my family. The series is 3-part. I was sure to include a title for Moms, Dads, and Stepparents, because I've found that the issues I help my clients work through are common based on their parental role.

This book was written for all fathers, whether a non-custodial parent or a single dad who is struggling with either making the transition into a divided family or struggling with co-parenting peacefully with their child's mother. Implementing some or all of the tips and practices mentioned in this book will help you not only resolve some of the problems you experience with your child's mom, but will also move you towards a life of peace. Now don't get me wrong. This book is not the cure-all to all of the problems you will experience, but it was written with the most common problems dads experience in mind. Some things will apply to you, some things will not. Some things will work, some will not. Some things you will feel are common sense and some things will lead you to a mental breakthrough. One thing is certain, this book will challenge you to look at the full picture of your situation. It will challenge you to evaluate your own actions, your child's mother's actions, and to consider everyone's feelings, perspectives, and/or expectations. At times, it will also challenge you to put your own frustrations in check and make adjustments as necessary in order to foster a peaceful relationship between you and your child's mother. It will guide you through different ways to co-parent peacefully and reduce the drama if possible, or properly resort to alternative action if absolutely necessary.

The key to gaining the most from this book is to be truthful with yourself. You have to face your *actual* reality, not just "your side of the story," that you have been conveying to everyone else, while omitting a lot of vital facts. You have to be both open-minded and willing to do the work. The level of peace our family gets to experience did not happen overnight. It took conscious effort and discipline.

Be forewarned, this book isn't for the faint of heart, as I am very direct and honest throughout - I do not sugarcoat the truth. However, you should understand that it is all love, albeit "tough love." I have a genuine interest in minimizing the problems that many fathers of divided families face so that children will have a better future. So many divided families are struggling to co-parent peacefully and the majority of the time it's because rather than looking at the full picture and seeking resolutions, both parties usually just play the blame game; accusing the other parent as being the reason their lives are filled with drama or why their relationship with their child is non-existent or in turmoil.

Although your child's mother could in fact be the

main reason that the two of you are unable to co-parent, it is highly likely that you are also part of the problem and simply do not realize it. While true co-parenting requires both of you to work together, a significant factor that influences your situation is *you*. Unfortunately you cannot control your child's mother, but you can control your own actions and reactions. Perhaps you are doing all the correct things already; maybe you have done everything in your power to make your co-parenting situation the best it can possibly be, but maybe not.

A large part of co-parenting effectively is based upon your mindset and how you handle situations as they arise. You have to learn to take control of the things that you can, and properly deal with the things you cannot control. Specifically, you must learn how to take control of your situation and recognize your responsibility, rather than impulsively blaming all of your problems on your child's mother. This can be very hard to get used to, especially if your child's mother has alienated you from your child, used your child against you, or otherwise caused problems in your life. But, it's not impossible. In fact, it's very simple once you change your mindset and your actions. It's a concept I like to call The Business of Co-Parenting; commitment to learning and implementing this business will improve your situation drastically. It's my sincere hope that by learning and implementing the strategies discussed in this book, your family won't have to go through what my family went through. But, if you're already going through it, it is also my hope that like my situation, your situation can drastically improve and you can experience the co-parenting peace you deserve.

Sincerely,

Merissa   V.   Grayson

INTRODUCTION

Statistics you should know:

Numerous studies have been conducted across decades on the effects living in a divided or blended family have on children. The unwavering consensus is – Children who live in divided or blended families face greater risks than their counterparts. Among other things, they are more likely to drop out of school, abuse drugs and alcohol, have greater and earlier sexual activity, experience incarceration and teenage pregnancy, and need psychological counseling.

But why? Why do children in divided/blended families face so many negative risks? It's not solely because their parents aren't together; there are several great children who come from divided/blended family homes. I believe that these risks are more likely to apply to children when their parents are on two separate pages, refuse to cooperate, and in essence, fail to protect the best interest of their children. I believe that with the right mindset and action, parents can ensure that their children evade these negative risks and thrive in spite of the fact that their parents live in two separate homes. So how do you accomplish this when you and the other parent are so far from the goal? By learning "The Business of Co-Parenting."

So, what exactly is The Business of Co-Parenting? I have discovered that the most effective way to manage your divided family and keep everyone and everything running smoothly is to manage it as if you were managing a business. Every well-established business has a Chief Executive Officer (CEO). In businesses where the CEO is acting alone, the CEO is undeniably the highest-ranking person, in charge of total management and control of the business. Typically, in most divided families, moms assume this role, because more often than not, they are the custodial parent. However, if a father insists upon being present and active in his child's life, this can essentially level the parenting field, and the mother must then work jointly with him as a parenting Partner. That's where you come in.

In order to master the business of co-parenting, you must establish a parenting Partnership and actively contribute to the responsibilities required by acting as a *joint* leader, director, and decision maker of your divided family. Using the tips in this book, as a parenting Partner, you will learn to take control of a negative or even non-existing co-parenting situation and redirect it into a more positive direction. Equally important, you will learn to handle your co-parenting relationship with your child's mother as a business Partnership. By taking the business approach, you will tactfully handle negative circumstances so you can clearly focus on the task at hand - to protect your most valuable "business asset"- your child.

The Business of Co-Parenting Explained:

Let me put things into a more clear perspective for you:

Imagine that at your current job (or in your current business) there's a two billion dollar business opportunity for you (a legal one that doesn't go against your personal morals of course); let's say, a "promotion" or "bonus." In order for you to obtain this bonus or promotion, the only thing you would have to do is perform your usual job duties while working with an assigned team and manager, and show that you're a good "team player." That sounds reasonable right? I mean, regardless of your current financial situation right now, I'm sure you could use an additional two billion dollars. I'm also sure, that if the possibility of this two billion dollar promotion or bonus were on the table in real life, you would do whatever, literally (within reason of course) to protect this two billion dollar deal and make sure it didn't fail. You would more than likely deal with ugly attitudes, extra-long hours, being overworked, excessive criticism, picking up the slack of lazy or incompetent team members or ungrateful managers, and much more, as long as at the end of the project, you were going to get paid. Ironically, you've probably already dealt with these types of things in your current or previous job just to ensure that you would remain employed, and could make just enough to pay your bills or live paycheck to paycheck.

I hope that you would agree that your child is worth much more than two billion dollars. So, considering what you've already dealt with in order to maintain something that is of no comparison when it comes to true value, ponder this: Your child's mother is your assigned team or manager. <u>Your child is that two billion dollar business deal</u>. **What are you willing to do to protect him or her?** From this point forward, this is the mindset you must maintain in order to master The Business of Co-Parenting. Dealing with your co-parenting relationship like a business Partnership, with a very valuable deal on the line, as opposed to dealing with it as a prior romantic or intimate relationship that didn't work out, the game changes. When problems or disagreements arise, which unfortunately are oftentimes unavoidable, you will have the tools to effectively resolve or minimize them. You will be proactive, communicate clearly and directly without sweating the small stuff, and will as a result be able to protect your child's interests by lessening the feelings of loss they may be experiencing.

I.

UNDERSTANDING THE DIVIDED RELATIONSHIP

In order to unlock the full potential of the business of co-parenting you must understand the divided relationship, be at peace within yourself, understand the dynamics of everyone else involved, how the circumstances affect them, and how to deal with them accordingly.

What happened?

What happened? At one point, the two of you were a happy duo; either as a cute couple who were in love, dating to see if you were meant to be, or a fun fling who enjoyed each other for a season. Either way, at some point things were different; you spent time together and actually enjoyed it! Then something happened. The person who you were once so in love with, spent so much time with, had so much fun with, and/or enjoyed so much, became just the opposite. Now, every time you have to deal with her, you instantly get irritated and can't help but shake your head and wonder: "What the _____ (fill in the blank accordingly) was I thinking?" "How the _____ did I get into this mess?" And to make matters worse, unlike when you first met, you now have a child with this person, so walking away and erasing her from your life is pretty much impossible unless you are completely comfortable with being a deadbeat. Your child either looks like her or has mannerisms that remind you of her that make you cringe, want to throw something, or even change their DNA sometimes! Sound familiar? Don't worry, you're not alone. In most cases, these are natural human emotions.

But why? Why did you have to be the one to have a child with someone that seems impossible to work with? How did things get to this point? The answer: because "Stuff Happens!" There's no such thing as a perfect life or relationship. People make mistakes, timing isn't always right, some people are afraid of commitment, some just don't want to commit, some don't want to be parents, some don't want to grow up yet, some didn't have positive role-models growing up, some need help, some are bitter, some are evil, some don't know how, some don't care. We ALL are humans...humans are flawed. You may be at fault for this happening, or you may not. And although at some point you will definitely need to address why this happened in order to lessen the chances of it happening in the future, your number one priority right now is not to figure out what happened, who's at fault, or why it happened. What's done is done, the past is the past. You don't have a time machine, you can't take back your relationship, and you definitely can't (and shouldn't want to) put your child back where he or she came from. The only thing you can do at this point, is change what's going on right now.

EVALUATE <u>YOUR</u> ACTIONS:

Where's your focus?

Are you still stuck on the things that have happened in the past?

ACTION STEP:

If you still dwell on things that happened between you and your child's mother in the past, your first action step is to shift your focus. Your number one priority at this very moment is to face the things that are happening today and figure out the "how":

How are you going to move past this relationship that didn't work, the drama and frustration that came with it, and into a co-parenting relationship that works for the best interest of your child?

Facing the Facts

❖ *Know Your Role: The Parenting Partner*

Although legally, child custody and support is not based upon the gender of the parents, typically, the mother is often the one that is assumed ultimately responsible for many things that occur in that child's life, unless the father establishes otherwise. Why is that? One reason could be the fact that maternity is undisputable. Paternity, on the other hand, can easily be disputed, and often is. If you, as a father, decide to deny paternity and disappear into thin air prior to taking a paternity test, guess who is left to care for the child alone? The mother! If paternity is established and you <u>choose</u> not to be involved in your child's life, guess who is left? The mother! And for many moms, this is their reality. Just look at the statistics: there is a disproportionate number of single moms compared to single dads. According to the U.S. Census Bureau, out of approximately 12 million single parent families in 2014, around 83% were headed by mothers.

On the other hand, I think another reason moms are often declared the parent primarily responsible for their child, is because they insist upon this responsibility. In many instances, moms forcibly take control of what happens with their child and for one reason or another, the father is not as adamant; he yields to the mother's commands.

One reason fathers commonly allow this control, is because they often don't realize that they have the right to be the responsible parent just as the mother has that right. Many fathers assume that because she is "mom," she automatically has the right to custody and control of their child. In theory, this is a reasonable notion. After all, traditionally most (not all) mothers assume the role of a mother by instinct and nature. It doesn't matter what stage a woman is at in her life, once she becomes a mother, she consciously and intentionally alters many aspects of her life, specifically her lifestyle and mindset, even before giving birth. Many fathers admittedly wait to make these adjustments until after the child is born. Many fathers don't assume the level of responsibility that mothers typically and automatically do, even in "traditional" families where the mom and dad are still together or married.

Trust me, it's not just you. If you were to survey all of the married (or even cohabiting couples with children you know) and ask them to describe each other's levels of parental responsibility, I'm certain the majority of them will admit that although the dads are involved and have some responsibilities, the mom is the caretaker and assumes the largest part of the parenting role. That's not necessarily a bad thing, it's just the way we (society) naturally operate as a family unit. This is nothing new; it's been the tradition for ages.

But, for those of us who are in a divided/blended family, there are a lot of things we don't have the luxury of doing according to "tradition." Our family structures aren't exactly "traditional." Consequently, your role as a dad is not as flexible as it would be if you and your child's mother were together, or at least on the same page when it comes to co-parenting. As a father in a divided family, you must work significantly harder to level the parenting field because:

1) You likely don't reside in the same home as your child's mother,

2) You have the additional burden of dealing with co-parenting woes that often come with the territory of being in a divided family, and

3) You must be proactive and take appropriate steps to establish and/or enforce your position.

This is where knowing your role becomes important. Understanding your role as an equal parenting Partner will influence a lot of what happens with your divided family. You will contribute to the type of relationship you build or do not build with your child's mother. You ultimately have a huge hand in whether your child will grow up fatherless or otherwise turn into a statistic or will instead grow up and experience a thriving relationship with both parents; a part of one loving, yet divided family.

❖ *You are still a family:*

Yes, I said "a family." And although this may be a little hard to fathom right now, it's your reality. First things first:

The fact is, although you and your child's mother are no longer in a romantic or intimate relationship, you are still a family. Your DNA chains have been joined to create your child who is a part of both of you. Whether you like it or not, you are eternally tied together, as your child now has family that stems from you and his or her mother. They have grandparents, aunts, uncles, cousins, siblings, and possibly even nieces and/or nephews that you may not even know. You are now part of a divided family unit that must peacefully work together until your child reaches 18 years old, and perhaps beyond.

Now, I know you are probably thinking: "How in the world am I supposed to consider myself to be a 'family' unit with someone whom I have so much anger, frustration, or other foul thoughts of?" "I can hardly stand looking at or talking to her, how am I supposed to consider her family!?" Well, I will tell you, it's definitely a skill to be mastered; it requires consistent dedication, understanding, compromise, and a level of *maturity* that many people are incapable of obtaining due to stubbornness, ignorance, or just plain old stupidity. But not you! You can tackle this, no problem. You *will* tackle this for your child. *By* reading this book you have taken a major step. You will master what I like to call, as mentioned in the Introduction, The Business of Co-Parenting - a method for co-parenting without the unnecessary drama. It all starts with your mindset. And believe it or not, it's one of the best gifts you can give to your child.

❖ *You Have More Influence Than You Know:*

<u>Co-Parenting Defined</u>

Co-parenting is a relationship between two parents who are not married, living together or otherwise in an intimate relationship, yet they work together with

9

one another to organize their child's daily life and activities to ensure that the child receives the most consistent lifestyle and discipline possible and to ensure that each parent is fully aware of and involved in all issues related to their child. Essentially, the goal is to ensure that both parents and the child are all on the same page, and function as one family unit despite being divided into two separate homes. Sounds complicated right? It can very well be, but it doesn't have to be. As I mentioned, successful co-parenting requires an unimaginable, inclined level of maturity. And chances are, there are some important things missing from your co-parenting arsenal that are needed for you to reach that level. You may feel that getting to a point where you and your child's mother are finally on the same page is far-fetched at this very moment. But, that's the purpose of this book; to help YOU. It all starts with you.

So here's the thing: despite your anger, frustration, or ill feelings towards each other, unless there is a legally established reason your child should not have a relationship with one of you, your child has a legal right to develop and maintain a loving, caring, and stable relationship with both you and their mother. Becoming a parent is a commitment that adults have to their children. This commitment has nothing to do with the relationship between the parents and should not be influenced by such. This is why a co-parenting "business" model mindset and developing a partnership with your child's mother is so important.

Even if your co-parenting relationship isn't there yet, by you making the leap into a business model mindset, you can drastically improve your situation, lessen the unnecessary drama, and hopefully encourage your child's mother to make a conscious effort to do the same. If not, at least you can rest assured knowing that you did your very best to try to establish a co-parenting Partnership and you will also have the tools needed to remedy a lot of unnecessary problems and confusion, and to enforce your rights to be an active parent in your child's life.

<u>Lead by example:</u>

The fact is: No matter how influential you are, you can't make people change, you can only change yourself. People are who they are and no matter what, that's not going to change until THEY decide that change is necessary. BUT…you can influence others to want to change by being an example. It starts with you. If you want someone to do something, do a great job at showing them how it's done.

EVALUATE <u>YOUR</u> ACTIONS:

Take a moment to examine your mindset:

- *Have you been treating your situation as though your child's mother is simply your "ex" or "baby mama" rather than a part of your family?*

- *Instead of insisting on your rights to equal parenting, have you accepted your child's mother's tendency to control what happens with your child?*

- *Have you ever contributed to unnecessary drama, when you should've taken a different action?*

ACTION STEP:

If you answered "yes" to any of these questions, your next action step is to put in work. Make the extra effort necessary to change the tone of your co-parenting relationship into that of a positive, cooperative one. Your relationship with your child's mother will not fix itself. To improve the quality of your co-parenting relationship, you must take initiative and you must be persistent. Otherwise you will remain in the place you are in right now, waiting for things to change as you watch the years of your child's life pass you by.

If you don't like the way things are going, you must take clear, tactful action based upon a well-informed "business" decision made by you, the Partner of your co-parenting business.

Far too often I hear fathers complain about their child's mother and what she does and does not do. For example:

- *She "won't allow me to see my child."*

- *She "doesn't answer the phone when I call to speak with my child."*

- *"When I see her, she always makes a scene and wants to argue."*

- *"She lies and spreads rumors about me."*

- *"She talks bad about me in front of my child."*

- *"She makes my child say bad things about me."*

Trust me, I've heard and even seen it all. My question to any father who makes these complaints is always: "What have you done to resolve these problems?" Sadly, most fathers admit to taking little or no action. This was commonly either due to feeling as though they had no recourse or simply because it was easier to ignore the problem without challenge. Although it may be easier,

13

nothing in life worth having comes easy. As previously mentioned, as a father in a divided family, you will have to work significantly harder than a father in a "traditional" family. This means that until you are able to establish a co-parenting Partnership, you may have to take necessary actions to level the parenting field.

I know this may be extremely difficult, especially if your child's mom is uncooperative. However, you aren't doing this for them, you are doing it for your child and yourself. In spite of everything, you have to deal with your child's mom until your child turns 18 years old. Now, don't get me wrong, even if you master the business of co-parenting, you will still face many obstacles, but, by shifting your approach, you will be able to tactfully and professionally find the most practical solutions, which will put you in a more favorable position than you are currently in.

Dealing with the Past

So, for one reason or another, your intimate relationship with your child's mother is over…now what? Many people think the natural solution to an ended relationship is to let it go and try to move on. Unfortunately, in most cases it's not that simple. While escape from fruitless relationships can be beneficial, almost always, one or both parties to the relationship are left without closure. Often, by the time we get out of these failed relationships, we have become so fed up that we think the simple solution is to just get out, get away, walk away, and all of the problems will disappear. Sorry to say, it doesn't work like that; the relationship ends, but unsettled feelings remain. You know, those feelings of anger, hate, blame, pain, disappointment, betrayal, bitterness, or in some cases, just complete sadness. I know, I know...you, as a man, "aren't caught up in your emotions like that." And while that may be true, these are all normal feelings that almost *everyone* in a divided family experiences at some point. Marjorie Howard said it best when she said "everyone in a blended family is broken." This is true for divided families that haven't necessarily blended yet as well. Man or not, it's highly unlikely you *planned* to father a child with a woman you aren't with and no woman has "be a single/unmarried mom" on her goal list. There definitely isn't a child who wants to grow up without their mom and dad together or otherwise missing one of their parents in their life. One of the most important things to understand about living in a divided/blended family is that for the best interest of you, your child, and their future, they must be dealt with appropriately.

What does "dealt with appropriately" mean? Well, it basically means that you must figure out how to "get over it." Whatever "it" is. You must deal with the past, rather than acting as though it never happened. Many parents come to me for help because they are experiencing many difficulties that they blame on the other parent. However, after working with them, I realize they are not innocent in the problems they are experiencing. They are contributing to the problems that continue to manifest because they still haven't dealt with the past or are still not over "it."

❖   As For You:

Getting "over it" doesn't mean that the feelings you have aren't justified or that dealing with them is going to be easy. Nor am I saying that you are at fault. However, what I am saying is: you have a child whose interests are at stake, therefore, it is imperative that you understand that regardless of what happened in your relationship with your child's mother, and how you currently *feel* about her, there is a bigger picture now. You have a child that you have to raise together. And dealing with the past and getting over "it" is one of the first steps to doing so successfully without causing drama or detriment to them. This is the first step to ensuring that your child is the least negatively impacted by the division, and that you will have a positive relationship with your child.

If your feelings toward your child's mother are still ill, then you are not yet "over it" and you need to acknowledge that. Now let me be clear, just because you may not *want* her (to be with her intimately), doesn't mean you are truly "over it." If you are still angry, sad, or hurt by whatever it is she did (or did not do), you are not over it. To be over it you must not only forgive her for whatever happened, you must forgive yourself if you think you are at fault, and you must be willing and able to put the past behind you and let it go. If you do not work to truly get over it, you are in a sense letting her actions control your happiness, which will in turn affect your child's happiness.

I understand this may be much easier said than done. When you put your trust into someone and are hurt by that person, you can't help but hold onto those ill feelings, it's a natural human instinct. If you made a mistake that set off the demise of your family, feelings of guilt are built-in with the consequences of that mistake. But, for the best interest of your child, holding on to those ill feelings and/or guilt is not an option because these feelings of pain, anger, embarrassment, and more tend to cloud your judgment and will make it virtually impossible to build a co-parenting Partnership for the best interest of your child. In order to truly get over the "it" in your past, you must identify it, admit it, evaluate it, and search within yourself for the solution to resolve it. While I do not have your specific answer or solution, I suggest that you honestly ponder this issue. You owe it to yourself and your child. It will help make you a better father.

❖   As For Her:

The most valuable information I can give you here is: *A little empathy goes a long way.*

One of the most important things you must keep in mind is that women and men are different; we do not think or act the same. It's been commonly reported that women are more "emotional" than men. While I'm no expert on the variations of "emotional intelligence," in my experience, these claims seem to be pretty accurate. By and large, the mothers in divided families that I work with seem to have a more difficult time dealing with the division than the fathers (or maybe they just aren't as good at hiding it). As a woman and mother myself, I definitely can relate:

Naturally, at some point, almost every girl has a fairytale vision in her mind that one day she will meet the man of her dreams, have children, and live happily ever after as one big happy family. I know most of my friends growing up and I did! I always pictured myself dating the love of my life, who would one day ask for my hand in marriage; we'd have a huge wedding, and once we were set in our careers we'd have our first child together, our family would grow over the years (I wanted at least five kids), and live happily ever after. Like many, I had no sense of reality or the fact that things rarely work out perfectly like the fairy-tales. There are so many things they forgot to tell us in those books, it's ridiculous! They forgot to tell us that every relationship has its problems and that some relationships will not last forever. They forgot to mention that in real life, you will likely discover that the one you thought was the "love of your life" is probably not. They didn't mention that at some point, in some relationships you realize you aren't a good fit for each other and the relationship ends. And they definitely didn't tell you what to do next......

Whether she admits it or not, in most cases, if a woman carries your child, deep down inside she desires to have a family; she wants it to work out between the two of you. Consequently, when things have happened in your past relationship that have interfered with the possibility of fulfilling this desire, if her feelings go without being seen, oftentimes this is where the real problems begin. Although we (women), often claim, pretend to be, or maybe even believe that we are "okay" after being disappointed or hurt by someone, the reality is that by nature, we thrive off of our relationships with others and are therefore not okay. Because of this, many times when a relationship ends without a mutual understanding, the mother is left trying to deal with the division and confusing emotions on her own, while the father moves on without difficulty. Though your initial point of view may be "that's her problem, not mine!" This view could very well lead to problems for you.

Feeling unsupported through a time of family division can be an extremely uncomfortable situation that can very quickly escalate out of control. Hear me when I say this:

If you choose to disregard "her problem", your choice will have significant bearing on the type of co-parenting relationship you have with her; it may perhaps be the determining factor of whether you will have "baby mama drama" or a cohesive co-parenting Partnership.

The good news is, there are actions you can personally take in an effort to minimize this unnecessary drama and level the parenting field. A lot of times, one thing we often overlook is another's need to be understood. We sometimes become so consumed in our own perception that we close our eyes to the needs of others. As people in general, one of the most frustrating things we experience in life is feeling like another does not appreciate, recognize, comprehend, or care about our feelings. While for one reason or another you may not actually "care" about your child's mother's feelings, one thing is for certain, in divided/blended families, a little empathy can go a long way and can even potentially influence change in the dynamic of your divided family, for the better. Just so we're clear, I'm not suggesting that you exhibit *sympathy* for your child's mother. There's a pretty significant difference between sympathy and empathy. Sympathy is defined as *harmony of or agreement in feeling*. Suggesting that you have sympathy for your child's mother would be unreasonable, as that would possibly insist upon you forcing feelings that don't exist. Empathy on the other hand, simply requires *the capacity to recognize emotions that are being experienced by another*. To take it even deeper, there are two types of empathy:

1. **Affective Empathy** - the ability to respond with an appropriate emotion to another's mental state, and

2. **Cognitive Empathy -** the ability to understand

another's perspective or mental state.

To induce a positive parenting Partnership, you must demonstrate compassion for your co-parenting relationship, and the need to shift it into a more cooperative state. This requires you to be empathetic to your child's mother's feelings. It may be surprising to know that accomplishing this is really not difficult at all; it simply entails you recognizing the emotions that your child's mother may be experiencing (specifically as they relate to your separation), making an effort to understand her, and responding with an appropriate emotion. For example:

The next time your child's mother verbally expresses her ill feelings for you (i.e. "I hate you," "You aren't a good father," etc.) rather than reciprocating the same negative energy as you normally would, surprise her; calmly ask her why she feels this way (even if you already know, still ask), and actually listen intently to her response. Listen to her without interrupting, and not for the purpose of rebutting her argument, but solely for the purpose of gaining an understanding of why she feels the way she does. When she is done talking, recognize that you have heard every word she said and respond in a manner that expresses your hope to move forward; apologize for anything you have done to make her feel the way she does (even if it was unintentional, you were unaware of it, don't agree that it was your fault, or don't fully understand her viewpoint), and emphasize the importance of you and her letting the past go so that you can have a good relationship for the benefit of your child. While doing this may not magically or instantly resolve the tension that exists, you will have accomplished many things with this simple act:

1) By asking her why she still has the ill feelings she does, you have given her the opportunity to vent. In case you didn't know, a lot of times, us women simply need a chance to get whatever is bothering us off our chest, for no other reason than to gain closure or relieve our heart from what remains there, unsettled;

2) By listening to her intently, without interruption, you have demonstrated your *effort* to get an understanding of the root of her problems rather than argue with her;

3) By apologizing for any of your actions that led to her ill feelings toward you, you have not necessarily admitted to fault, but you have set an example of accepting accountability.

Although your child's mother may not positively

respond immediately, she will think about your approach and take it into consideration. By not responding to her in a combative way, you will open the door to peace moving forward. As previously mentioned, every suggestion written in this book is something that I've implemented in either my own personal life and/or profession. This is just one of the exercises I walk my coaching clients through. Trust me, the more efforts *you* make to improve the rapport between you and your child's mother, the better she will be able to deal with the past, and the less problems you will have in the future. A little empathy goes a long way.

❖ As For Your Parenting Partnership:

Emotional Ties & Counseling:

As mentioned before, everyone in a divided/blended family is broken. This includes you and/or your child's mother, and your child. Someone was likely hurt due to the division of your family. At one point, you thought the two of you were cool and on the same page, but for one reason or another, that wasn't the case. One of you lied, cheated, broke a promise, left, or otherwise played the other for the fool and as a result, one and/or both of you are hurting. You may feel disappointed, betrayed, sad, confused, embarrassed, or just straight up pissed off! You may wonder "what happened?" "Why would they do this?" "Who is this person?" You may even blame yourself at times, wondering, "How in the world did I not see this coming?" "What was I thinking?" Sometimes you think you'll be okay and just move on, other times you may question whether you'll ever be able to move on. Although you may outwardly be good at putting on a good front in order to fool everyone else into believing this doesn't faze you, deep down inside you may still be experiencing negative feelings toward each other that you think may never go away.

If any of the above sounds familiar, don't worry, the feelings you are experiencing are normal! When a family divides, ill feelings are expected; to expect anything less would be unrealistic. The first step to overcoming these feelings is to be honest with yourself. In order to move on from pain, hurt, or other ill feelings toward someone, you must first acknowledge that there is a problem; acknowledge within yourself that you are still emotionally hindered from this situation.

So, how do you collectively "get over it" once and for all? Well, the first thing you must understand is that it takes time. By no means will this happen overnight. Especially if one of you are "over it" and the other is not, or if one of you admit that you're still struggling with the events of the past, while the other is still in denial. However, I am a strong believer in one thing that may speed up the process, yet so many people are quick to decline - counseling. I know, I know, you "don't need counseling." Maybe you don't, but maybe you do, or maybe your child's mother does.

Counseling

There are so many common misunderstandings and misconceptions about counseling. For some reason, so many people are caught up on the misguided idea that counseling is only for those who are "crazy," or those with a mental illness, depression, extreme grief, or those going through unimaginable, traumatizing events. No one wants to believe that their situation rises to the level of a need for counseling because of the negative connotations associated with it.

Unfortunately, false perceptions about what counseling is, how it works, and who it's designed for often keep those who will likely benefit from it the most from considering it for themselves. Before you completely dismiss the idea of counseling, you should know that many people in a divided or blended family will need some counseling at some point, including your children; it's one of the many things that come with the territory needed to resolve the brokenness that divided and blended families experience. The fact is that counselors are professionals who assist people with many different aspects of life, not just those who are ready to jump over the edge. There are hundreds of types of counselors, each with their own specialty, serving their own chosen population. While it is true that some counselors do work with those who have severe mental illnesses, disorders, addictions, etc., there are numerous counselors across the globe who work with people dealing with everyday issues such as their careers, education, marriages, parenting, and health. Counseling can be a very good resource. It gives you a chance to talk over what is on your mind with a neutral person who can help you explore and understand the happenings in your life and teach you new skills and ways of looking at life so that you will be more capable of solving problems on your own. Whenever I get a new client, one of the first things I consider as part of their legal or coaching plan is counseling. Many of my clients are initially reluctant to enroll, but it never fails, those who follow the suggestion to at least give it a try, later admit that it was one of the best decisions they made and that it gave them great headway towards healing and progress.

If you are still finding yourself struggling with any of the emotional aspects of your situation, or if you believe your child's mother may be struggling with the same, counseling is something you should definitely consider. Also, if your child is having difficulty with the transition to a divided family, blended family, or a newly established or reconciled relationship with you, you should definitely consider counseling for them.

The bottom line is, being a part of a divided family is not naturally easy, especially for the parents. And if it's not easy for the parents, the ones in control, imagine how the children feel. This may be one of the most complicated things that you will have to do because there are so many different people involved, with so many different personalities, mindsets, and points of view. But, it can be easy. If you put in the work, you can make your life less difficult than it is or needs to be. In order to unlock the potential of the business of co-parenting so that you can live in peace, you must set a solid foundation; to do so you must not only be at peace within yourself, but you must also understand the dynamics of your divided/blended family, how the circumstances affect everyone involved, how to manage them accordingly and hopefully instill peace into your divided family as a whole. In order to achieve this, you must deal with the past and set goals for the future. Again, The Business of Co-parenting is not something that comes naturally; it is a skill, a much defined one that will hopefully develop into a lifestyle.

Family Ties, Courses, and Coaching

Speaking of coaching, if you continue to struggle to effectively co-parent with your child's mother due to high conflict or non-cooperation on her part, self-help books such as this one may suffice. However, if you need a little more hands-on guidance or help incorporating the principles in this book into your life, you may want to consider a live co-parenting course or a life coach.

There are many different types of co-parenting courses offered throughout the country. In many high conflict cases, some judges will require parents to complete these courses as part of a court order. Some courses are available for the parents to attend individually, while others require the parents to attend together. Courses are often short term (usually no more than a few weeks) and may be conducted in either a small or large group setting and allow parents to openly discuss and learn solutions to issues that are common amongst divided families.

In contrast, a life coach is a professional who helps clients set and achieve personal goals. A co-parent coach is a life coach whose job is to help you identify and take tactful action toward goals for your divided family. A coach will work with you individually or with both you and your child's mother, by getting to know you, helping enhance the things that you are doing well, and adjust the areas that are not working or which can be done better. In a sense, a co-parent coach can serve as a facilitator in helping you accomplish your full parenting potential despite your differences and difficulties with your child's mother. Unlike counseling, the emphasis of coaching is not placed on what has happened in the past; coaching is geared towards your present circumstances, thoughts and actions and how to shift them in order to positively impact your future. Because your coach will fully understand your concerns and ultimate goals, he or she will refer you to other resources or professionals, such as a counselor, if necessary.

EVALUATE <u>YOUR</u> ACTIONS:

Take a moment to truthfully think about your feelings.

- *Are you still struggling with ill feelings towards your child's mother?*

- *Do you still have feelings of anger, blame, hate, disappointment, betrayal, pain, sadness, or bitterness?*

- *Do you still have intimate feelings for her or a desire to be intimately involved with her that are interfering with your ability to move on? Rather than truly being "over it," are you still holding on?*

- *Does your child's mother still express any of the above toward you?*

ACTION STEP:

If you answered "yes" to any of these questions, it's okay. After all, these feelings are a normal reaction to a relationship that didn't work out. What's not okay is either of you holding onto these feelings without acknowledging them. So, your next action step is to acknowledge that it's time to take control of both your feelings and your mindset. If you find yourself struggling with your own emotions, you should look into your intervention options. Now is the time to take whatever steps are necessary to do what you need to do in order to finally be at peace with what happened, forgive your child's mother and/or yourself, and completely let go and move on. If your

31

child's mother is the one who refuses to let go, it's time to put that empathy I talked about into play. If that doesn't aid in a positive shift, you may want to consider gently suggesting counseling for your family and see if she'll go for it. Keep in mind that a good business Partner knows when to seek outside resources when the internal resources are not working.

II.

UNDERSTANDING HER

One of the key aspects to the business of co-parenting is understanding your co-parent; in your case, the type of mother you are dealing with and her probable perspective on the overall divided family and her role in it.

Now, in no way am I suggesting that you should always agree with your child's mother's actions or even her perspective, but...by understanding, you can make informed decisions on how to manage your divided family more effectively based on your circumstances. Remember, you can't change someone else, but you can change the way you deal with them and lead by example. While no two mothers are exactly the same, in divided families, I notice there tends to be a common trend; four different "categories" of mothers: 1) The Present Mother, Absent Lover; 2) The Woman Scorned; 3) The "Irrational Mom;" and 4) The Deadbeat. The type of mother she is will likely influence her perspective, her tendencies, and in turn the best way to interact with her in an effort to create a harmonious divided/blended family.

Present Mother (Absent Lover)

Although you and your child's mother are no longer intimately involved with each other, the present mother, absent lover, still has a genuine interest in being the best mom she can. If you are dealing with the present mother, you should consider yourself to be one of the luckiest dads on earth. She pretty much just wants to be "mom" regardless of what's happened or happening between the two of you. You may not always see eye to eye and you may feel like you're never "on the same page." But the truth is, you could have it *way* worse. Imagine experiencing so much consistent drama and chaos when trying to maintain a relationship with your child, that you feel the only way to escape it is to disappear and not have a relationship at all. Many fathers cite never-ending high conflict with their child's mother as one of their biggest problems. This is often the case for fathers who have been absent or minimally involved in their children's lives; many reported that when faced with the choice between being in their child's life and consumed with drama and being absent, but drama-free, they chose the latter. While I don't believe this is a good enough reason to sacrifice a relationship with your child, because I personally identify with divided family conflict that gets out of control, I can see how a parent may feel like the only way to protect their child from the adverse effects of the same, and live in peace would be to walk away and terminate the drama altogether. Luckily, the present mother, absent lover isn't interested in drama. It doesn't matter how you feel about her, how she feels about you, or what happened in your relationship; that is no longer of concern. The only thing she is focused on is protecting the interests of her child and ensuring that her child has the best future possible. So, if your child's mother falls into this category, getting to a place of peace and cooperation when it comes to co-parenting won't be as challenging as you think. A few tweaks in your mindset and the way you handle your dealings and you'll be well on your way to the drama-free life you desire.

Problems with her will likely arise if you are struggling with facing the past, learning how to deal with the loss of the relationship, or understanding her perspective. Now, don't get me wrong, she is far from perfect. Just like you, she makes mistakes and bad decisions from time to time, but all in all, she is a good mom and simply wants the best for your child. She ultimately wants you to spend time with your children, love them, have fun with them, teach them, guide them, support them, provide for them, and be involved in almost every aspect of their lives. Notwithstanding her positive outlook, worry caused by previous interactions with you may impede these desires if they have not yet been dealt with. This is why dealing with the past is so important. Once the two of you have tackled your unresolved issues, the present mother, absent lover has the potential to be the best mother to co-parent with.

EVALUATE YOUR ACTIONS:

If you are experiencing difficulty co-parenting with a present mother (absent lover):

- *Have you addressed the past in effort to prevent it from interfering with your relationship with your child? (See Chapter I.)*

- *Have you sincerely tried co-parenting with her?*

ACTION STEP:

If you answered "no" to either of these questions, there's a great chance that you are contributing to many of the problems that you are experiencing. Your action step is to make a conscious effort to establish a parenting Partnership with your child's mother. Take steps beyond those that you would

normally take to level the parenting field.

So how do you accomplish this? Firstly, you must remember to remain focused on the task at hand: co-parenting for the best interest of your child. Regardless of how you feel about your child's mother, negative interaction with her is not good for your child, especially if done in his or her presence or within hearing distance. This goes back to the importance of "getting over it." Although important to you, issues outside of those related to your child are not a part of co-parenting. If your child's mother doesn't want to be involved with you intimately, she doesn't have to. If she doesn't want to discuss your past relationship, she doesn't have to, and vice versa. Her role as your child's mother no longer has anything to do with your past relationship, but everything to do with your child. Yes, I understand that this may be very frustrating and may leave you in an uncomfortable position, especially if you haven't hashed out the issues you have with her. However, they have counseling, coaching, courses, programs and books to help you deal with that. You have an important goal that must be met for the best interest of your child - mastering the business of co-parenting, so you can live drama free.

Secondly, YOU must take the initiative to develop a

strong bond with your child and a positive relationship with your child's mother. Make an effort to spend quality time with your child on a regular basis. Make an effort to remain informed of the happenings in your child's life and to take part in the decision-making process as much as possible. Communicate with your child's mother regularly regarding your child and without forcing undesirable conversations on her that are unrelated to co-parenting. Attend as many events or programs your child is a part of, and be cordial when you see your child's mother. The better relationship you have with your child's mother, the better relationship you will have with your child. (More ideas and tips are available in Chapters III. and V.)

The Woman Scorned

The woman scorned is probably one of the most confusing moms to deal with. She falls somewhere in between the present mother, absent lover, and the irrational mom (discussed below). She has a genuine interest in being a good mother to her child, but *you* on the other hand, are on her "s%$# list." Consequently, although you can rest assured that your child will always be well taken care of, if you don't make a serious effort to nip the problems she has with you in the bud, your co-parenting relationship will likely be extremely uncomfortable, as her attitude towards you will remain unpredictable.

A mother becomes "The woman scorned" due to unresolved issues tied to your previous relationship with her. She has been lied to, cheated on, deceived, or otherwise disappointed and doesn't necessarily know how to handle these emotions. The good news is, if you take a positive step toward resolving the unsettled issues with her directly, she can transition into the present mother, absent lover. The bad news is, if these unsettled issues remain as-is, there's a great chance that she can adversely transition into "the irrational mom."

So, how do you co-parent with a woman scorned? Well, the key to turning your co-parenting relationship with her around goes back to the discussion in Chapter I., dealing with the past and your attitude towards what you normally may consider to be "her problems." In many situations, the mother remains the woman scorned because her feelings about issues related to your former relationship have been ignored as if they never occurred and don't matter. Just because you ignore your past, doesn't mean it goes away. The fact still remains that whatever happened between you and her may still be hindering your ability to move forward. Remember, hurt people, hurt people. A great first step to remedying this situation is to try to lessen the hurt that your child's mother may be experiencing. Try the exercise described in Chapter I., while also consciously making additional efforts to change the dynamic of your divided family. The idea remains, a little empathy can go a long way.

The Irrational Mom (a.k.a. "Crazy Baby Mama")

Irrational, selfish, not concerned about the welfare or best interests of her child, unreasonable, with an agenda centered on vengeance and making your life miserable. Sound familiar? This is the irrational mom (also known as "The Crazy Baby Mama"). When I'm contacted by a father who needs help resolving issues related to his divided family, the most commonly cited problem is a "crazy baby mama."

Although oftentimes people nonchalantly refer to some mothers as the "crazy baby mama," more often than not, there is nothing crazy about her at all. When asked why she is "crazy," answers given usually describe a woman scorned or the present mother, absent lover. A woman does not automatically qualify as a "crazy baby mama" simply because she disagrees with you, doesn't want to be in a relationship with you, has ill feelings towards you, doesn't get along with you, or *justifiably* (←key word) won't allow you to see your child. After all, certain circumstances create logical reason for all of these things. As far as I'm concerned, every mother that's being labeled as a "crazy baby mama" will initially get the benefit of the doubt. But, there are certain actions that would make one undeserving of that benefit, and may reasonably justify a belief that the mother is in fact a "crazy baby mama."

Now, before I get too deep into this, let me first disclaim that *I personally despise the use of the term "baby mama" in real life. So, when you see it used herein, understand, that I am not encouraging use of the term to refer to your child's mother; the use within this book is solely for dramatic effect and quoting purposes.*

Almost everyone knows at least one "irrational mom;" whether she is in fact your child's mom, a relative, close friend, or just someone you are acquainted with. She is the mom that refuses to let go of the past and consciously puts her own emotions before the best interest of her child. Suffering from emotional instability, she oftentimes makes decisions based on her emotions at a particular moment, without regard to how it will affect her child's future. Consequently, in some instances she will alienate her child from his or her father, abuse her child, neglect her child, and sometimes worse just to "get back at" the father of her child. This makes her not only the most frustrating and complicated mom to deal with, but in some cases, also the most dangerous.

Domestic Violence & the Abusive Mom

One reason it's so important that you are careful in your approach when dealing with an irrational mom, is because irrational moms who get out of control may take outrageous action against you and/or your child, commonly related to domestic violence. Unfortunately, at some point, many families experience domestic violence issues. Some families experience domestic violence and do not even realize it. This is especially true in light of the fact that many people have a false belief of what behavior rises to the level of domestic violence and whether domestic violence can actually be perpetrated by a female. Having an abusive mom (or anyone for that matter) involved in you or your child's life can become a very dangerous situation. Just So You Know: Domestic Violence is broadly defined as a pattern of abusive behaviors by one or both partners in a domestic relationship.

A relationship is considered domestic if it is between family members, romantic partners, or the parents of a child. Abuse is not limited to physical actions, but it includes any emotional or psychological behaviors that hurt, frighten, humiliate, intimidate, terrorize, manipulate, or blame someone. This type of abuse is the most common form of abuse perpetrated by irrational moms, as they often influence their children on how to feel and/or act toward their dad through manipulation and intimidation.

If you have reason to believe that you or your child is a victim of domestic violence, the best thing you can do is to get help sooner than later. Many fathers' situations become so extreme that their most immediate resolution is to protection by filing an Application for a Domestic Violence Restraining Order. A Domestic Violence Restraining Order is basically a legal injunction that requires a party to do or not do certain acts. Orders to turn over firearms, stay within a certain distance of you or your child, attend anger management/domestic violence classes, or mandatory classes to help recover from drug and alcohol abuse are just a few of the remedies that a restraining order may include. The length of time that the order is in effect, and the scope of protection are determined by the court. One who refuses to comply with a domestic violence restraining order can face criminal or civil penalties.

Even in situations where the children are not victims, if the court orders a restraining order against a parent to protect the other parent, the restrained parent's rights to their children will be severely affected because as a result, in some jurisdictions, there is an automatic presumption that they should not have custody of their child.

Beware: This sometimes becomes a tactic for some irrational moms. Many irrational moms will fabricate allegations against their child's father in an effort to prevent his rights to custody of their child. Sadly, in cases like these, the mother will claim everything from the child not wanting to visit with the father, to the father physically and/or sexually abusing the child, to the father threatening to physically harm the mother. She will say anything in an effort to secure a restraining order against the father and ultimately interfere with his custody and visitation rights.

If you feel that your child's mother is so extremely irrational that it will be impossible to establish a peaceful relationship with her, don't fret yet. Believe it or not, it is very possible for an irrational mom to transition into the absent lover, present mother. Notice that I said **transition**; this is not something that will happen overnight. In fact, it is a process that could take months or even years and will likely require a lot more effort on your part than you prefer to contribute. However, if you are determined to protect the welfare and best interest of your child, you can significantly change your divided family relationship. The key to dealing with an irrational mom is tactful action; the way you approach every situation will likely have great influence on the outcome of that situation.

Fighting the Fire

Have you ever heard the saying, "you can't fight fire with fire"? Well, that phrase isn't to be interpreted literally. After all, in actuality you can fight fire with fire; it's done by professionals all the time. Once, while watching the news there was a huge story about an out of control fire that spread throughout one of the major Canyons in Southern California. The fire was spreading so rapidly due to high wind speeds that the standard methods normally used to put out fires were unsuccessful. So, specialists decided to use more advanced methods, including what they refer to as "back burning," a method of controlled burning. The idea of "back burning" is that by intentionally starting small fires along the main fire front, the small fires will burn back towards the large fire that is out of control and in essence, little flammable material will exist by the time the fire reaches the burnt area.

So what's the point? You can't successfully fight fire without specific skill and *intention*. It would never be wise to just go recklessly starting fires simply because another fire is out of control and expect to resolve the problem. The key to fighting a fire with fire is that in order to do so successfully, you must be a "professional," a "specialist." You must be tactful. This same principle should be applied in real life encounters with others, especially your child's other parent. If you don't like the way things are going, change what you can. The analogy to fire-fighting and co-parenting like a CEO is that, as a professional, reasonable parent, there will be times when changing your strategy is necessary in order to put out the fire you are dealing with.

For example, there was one man whose ex-wife was so distraught that the marriage ended, she became extremely irrational. She did everything within her power on a quest for vengeance to make his life miserable; everything from alienating their child from him, using the child as a pawn, obtaining a restraining order against him by making false allegations of threats made against her, defaming him, and even stalking him. Understandably, his

47

first inclination in reaction to her behavior was outrage. Instead, he took the approach of a professional parent; he sought legal counsel, had the false charges dropped, established official orders for child custody, and secured a restraining order against her as well as an order that she seek counseling and anger management classes. Although he didn't stoop to her level and respond in an irrational manner, he also did not sit idly by and endure her behavior without taking any action at all. In my uncontrollable fire example above, when the city couldn't stop the fire from spreading, they changed their approach; they brought in a professional whose specialty is "back burning." Similarly, when this husband's situation got out of hand, he fought fire with fire by acting as a professional co-parent, tactfully taking control of his situation.

You must learn to be and think of yourself as a professional parent, whose specialty is The Business of Co-Parenting for the best interest of your child, even in difficult situations. While you can't change your child's mom's behavior or the fact that she is your child's mom, you can shift *your* mindset. Be the "back burner": Think about what YOU can do differently to influence change. If someone you are dealing with is combative and always wants to argue and fight, don't take part in it. Refuse to participate in any quarrels and let the person know how to reach you when they are done arguing with themselves. If you want to be respected, show respect. If you want consideration, show some consideration. And remember that change happens for others when THEY are ready. It's not going to happen overnight. But if you constantly greet someone who's combative with a generous smile (no matter how much you'd rather just tell them where to go), eventually they won't have a choice but to smile back. Any other responsive behavior would simply make them appear psychotic for continuing to argue with themselves.

With this in mind, although you can't change your child's mom's behavior, you must take the appropriate, tactful steps that will influence her to change herself. If she needs counseling or some other type of professional help, you must figure out the best way to ensure that either 1) she gets the help she needs or 2) her failure to get this help does not detrimentally affect the best interests or well-being of your child. The hardest part about dealing with the irrational mom is figuring out the most practical approach you should take in order to accomplish this task. Because there is obvious tension in your relationship with her, she is not likely to accept advice or suggestions about her coping needs from you. Perhaps you can seek the assistance of someone who is close to her to help her understand that counseling or some other type of intervention would be beneficial for her in dealing with the dynamics of the divided family.

As you can see, there are many different directions a divided family relationship with an irrational mom can take. Your goal is to find and take the most practical road that will ultimately lead to safety and peace. Depending on the severity of her irrationality and your circumstances, this may require seeking help from a lawyer, the Department of Children and Family Services/Child Protective Services, and/or the court system. Consequently, the success of your personal efforts and said interventions will influence whether she will transition from irrational to the absent lover, present mother, or will diminish to a deadbeat.

The Deadbeat Mom

Although people rant and rave about "deadbeat" dads all the time, very seldom do we hear about "deadbeat" moms. Naturally, when someone refers to a deadbeat parent, it's automatically presumed to be the dad; many people are still very surprised to learn that there is a such thing as a "deadbeat" mom. This unawareness is likely due to the fact that there is such a high percentage of single moms when compared to the percentage of single dads. Notwithstanding this, more and more fathers are taking care of their children with little or no help from the mother now than ever before.

❖ *Deadbeat Defined*

Regardless of the gender we are speaking of, in my opinion, the term "deadbeat" is overused and misused. Whenever I hear someone call a parent a deadbeat, I usually ask: "What makes them a deadbeat?" The overwhelming response is always some variation of "because they don't have any money or pay child support." Huh? Is that it? Because they can't or don't pay you money, that makes them a deadbeat? Confused by this, I decided to look up the term 'deadbeat' to get a better understanding of the term. To my surprise, definitions I found were almost identical to the common responses I received. Most legal definitions of a "deadbeat" included references of a "parent who fails to pay child support."

Let me be clear, I understand that finances are important, however, considering the fact that being a parent requires much more important characteristics than "having money," I find this to be an absurd definition that is completely unfair because the definition is extremely broad and insensitive of specific circumstances. There are so many different circumstances that can lead to one's failure to pay child support. Specifically, and most commonly, Stuff Happens! Life is not perfect. Sometimes a parent may genuinely, temporarily be unable to afford to make substantial financial contributions to their child's life. With the history of our economy, even those with higher education and years of work experience are finding themselves unemployed, underemployed, or otherwise struggling to make ends meet. Does this mean that parent should be labeled a "deadbeat" or not be able to see their child because of their financial situation? Absolutely not! If that were the case, there would be a ridiculous increase in the amount of children who are parent-less because financial problems affect both mothers and fathers. Automatically deeming one who does not pay child support (irrespective of specific circumstances, including any other contributions made to their child's life) a deadbeat is shallow and ridiculous.

Let's look at it another way, what about the parents who do contribute financially, but that is all they do? Is that enough? People tend to forget that it takes much more than money to raise a child. A parent can pay all the money in the world in child support and still be a deadbeat. Society has us so wrapped up in riches and material things that we often disregard what is more important. Yes, it does take money to raise a child: children need food, clothing, shelter, and other necessaries of life. However, a child who has the necessaries of life, but does not have the time, attention, love and support they need from their parents is a lost child. Even if a parent is unable to provide financially, they should be able to contribute to their child's life in other aspects without being labeled a deadbeat. There are plenty of parents who may be struggling financially, yet are phenomenal parents.

I believe we should all re-define the word "deadbeat." My definition of a "deadbeat" is: **one who deliberately fails to provide financial support for their child and/or refuses or fails to make reasonable efforts to be involved in their child's life as a parent.** In other words, someone who willingly and completely abandons his or her child.

So, what do you do if you find yourself in the position of a single dad because your child's mother is a deadbeat? Although my core suggestion on improving the dynamic of your divided family thus far has been to focus on what *you* can do to influence change in your situation, unfortunately, a true deadbeat mom may not be easily influenced. After all, being a deadbeat is *not* natural, for a man or a woman - but especially not for a woman. For most parents, once their child is born it is natural to want to be a parent to that child regardless of the circumstances. Even those who "did not want" kids more often than not become loving parents after the fact; they soon learn that it is no longer about what they want, but what's best for their child that now exists whether they wanted the child or not. Considering this, it's safe to say that unfortunately, if a person has entered into true "deadbeat" status, there is a great chance that he or she will remain there indefinitely.

Although in ideal situations a deadbeat mom will have a "change of heart," "find herself," or whatever else needs to happen for her to transform into that of an active parent, this doesn't always happen. With that being said, life must go on, with or without her. You and your child do not have time to wait until she's *ready* and it would be unreasonable to expect you to. The good news is that when it comes to co-parenting, unfortunately and fortunately, the deadbeat is the easiest type of mother to deal with because you don't really have to co-parent with her. True deadbeats are never (or hardly ever) around. The highest level of involvement (if any) that you will have from her in your life is that of paying child support as ordered and maybe an occasional visit. In many instances, you are able to maintain complete control of your child's life. The deadbeat does not care about making decisions related to your child, does not visit with your child, and your child may not even know she exists. The bad news is that regardless of what she does or doesn't do, you still have a child to take care of financially, physically, and emotionally.

Of course no one wants to deal with a deadbeat, but unfortunately you may in fact be in a situation in which you are forced to. Instead of dwelling on your child's mom's absence, focus on your presence as a single parent and take this opportunity to take on dual roles as both father and "mother." We all know that women are typically more emotional than men. Considering that, I suggest you make a real effort to think outside the box of a typical man and try to provide your child with more emotional support than you normally would. You may need to seek advice from the women in your life, but it's worth the effort. Your child will miss nurturing from his or her mother so you will have to provide that support.

Many single parents make the mistake of believing that because their child "seems fine," they must in fact not have any qualms about their other parent's absence. Surprisingly, this is not always the case. Often, upon gaining the understanding that their biological parent *willingly* chose not to be an active and present parent in their life, children experience a wide realm of feelings. These feelings can range from that of emptiness, frustration, anger, confusion, sadness, and more. For this reason, it's important to be aware that even if your child seems content, and even if he or she has another mother figure in his or her life, he or she may silently dwell on troubling emotions regularly. Be sensitive to this possibility and be as proactive as possible by communicating with your child regularly and expressing your love and support. Take action as necessary to help your child cope with any disconcerting feelings he or she may be experiencing, in an effort to prevent it from hindering the future.

III.

OUT WITH THE OLD, IN WITH THE NEW

So now that you and your child's mother have separated, there are a lot of new adjustments that everyone in your divided family must make. It's important to put your personal feelings aside in order to make decisions that are in your child's best interest.

57

New Habits

When a child is born, the lives of the parents (the active ones that is) change drastically. Things no longer revolve solely around the parents' wants or desires, but rather tend to lean more towards what is best for the family as a whole. When two parents are married or cohabiting, things typically tend to function much differently than when they are separated. When parents live together, the opportunity to share in all of the child's time and child-rearing decisions is more readily available, because as a part of the parents' relationship, they likely, *naturally* work together as a team to ensure that their family functions as a solid unit.

Unfortunately, when parents separate, this natural inkling to work together as a team gets lost in the division of the family; each parent begins to focus on what they need to do as an individual to move on from the relationship and thrive as a single person. The needs of your child cannot be lost at the conclusion of your intimate relationship with his or her mother; it's even more important now that you step your parenting game up to make sure this doesn't happen. With division comes a lot more responsibility and as a father of a divided family, you must realize said responsibilities to protect the best interest of your child. Things can no longer revolve around your personal desires without consideration of and adjustments for your child as needed. In other words, it's time to get rid of a lot of old habits and bring in the new.

❖ P.U.S.H. Through The Deadbeat Zone

Previously I discussed deadbeat moms, now I ask, Are you a deadbeat dad? You don't have to answer that. If you are a deadbeat dad, let's see how we can change that. In my experience, I've met and worked with so many distressed fathers who were not actively involved in their child's lives nearly as much as they wanted to be. While reasons for their absence varied, many of them complained that it was impossible to be involved because they constantly had to deal with drama such as being faced with constant questions not related to the child, false accusations of abuse, threats to keep the child away, and in some instances just straight up degrading, disrespectful remarks from the child's mother. Others admitted to being absent because at the time their child was born, they were "not ready" for a child. Some claimed their absence was not their choice, but that they were denied the opportunity to establish and maintain a relationship with their child by their child's mother. Regardless of the reason, a father's absence from his child's life can be detrimental to that child.

Fatherless children are at a dramatically greater risk of:

- drug and alcohol abuse.

- lower academic performance

- violent behavior

- the need for psychological counseling

- suicide

- and much more!

So, no matter how much some may try to diminish the importance of fathers, the fact is that children need their fathers; when they grow up fatherless, they face far greater negative risks than their counterparts and when they grow up with their fathers who have a strong presence and positive relationship with them, they benefit.

Absent fathers are often automatically put into the "deadbeat" zone, whether he deserves to be there or not. The bad news is once you're in the deadbeat zone, getting out will be a journey full of twists and turns, to say the least. The good news is there *is* a way out.

If you have found yourself in the deadbeat zone, don't fret. The key factor that will determine whether you will ever be able to establish and/or rebuild and maintain a positive relationship with your child is your commitment to doing so. Because there may be a battle against you, you must be willing to take calculated actions in order to exert your parental rights. Sadly, this is a battle that many are not willing to fight, as it requires: **P**ersistence, **U**rgency, **S**elflessness, and **H**ealing.

Persistence is key because you may not achieve the results you seek the first go-round, the second, or even the third. Factors such as the reason you have been absent, the length of your absence, the relationship that is or is not already established with your child, your child's wishes, etc. are all things that will likely influence the transition out of the deadbeat zone. For example, if your absence is the result of alienation caused by your child's mother, you may get out of the deadbeat zone sooner than if you purposefully chose to abandon your child due to the happenings of your life at that particular time. Not to say that the latter would make it impossible for you to build/re-build a relationship with your child, but it may take longer.

This is where *Urgency* comes in. The only way that you will push through the deadbeat zone is if doing so is important to you. Developing a better relationship with your child can no longer only be something you think about or want. It must become a necessity. If not, the first opposition that you face will cause you to become discouraged or throw in the towel. As previously mentioned, you will likely be up for a battle. It's up to you to prepare for that battle. What are you willing to do and/or endure so that you can win, for your child? If you think it's going to be a walk in the park, chances are, you are up for a rude awakening.

For this reason, it's imperative that you understand and take on the characteristic of *Selflessness*. The bad news is, if you are in the deadbeat zone, chances are, you have not yet learned the art of selflessness. Selflessness would not allow you to abandon your child because you "weren't ready" to be a parent or "can't deal" with your child's mother due to her being irrational. Selflessness wouldn't allow you to concede to your child's mother's interference with your relationship with your child. If you don't have a relationship with your child, the lack of a relationship ultimately lies on you because even if your child's mother refuses to "allow" you to see your child, there are definitely remedies available to resolve that problem. The good news is, you're reading this book, which will hopefully lead you to a remedy, starting with the act of selflessness. Selflessness is defined as *putting someone else's needs, interests, or wishing before your own.* In essence, selflessness will require you to make a lot of sacrifices. I suggest that you become more assertive and insist – in a positive way – that you are provided with more time with your child. Show your child's mother that you are dependable and reliable. Begin with baby steps in developing or re-developing a relationship with your child. Visit with your child a few times per week if possible and increase the time appropriately.

You will have a lot of moments where you may experience discomfort, frustration, anger, sadness, happiness, anxiety, and more. The key here is to know why you are going through this battle. You have to remember that it's not necessarily about you, it's about your child. Your child is depending on you to push through the deadbeat zone and into the equal parenting zone so that they may enjoy your presence in their life. Your ability to be selfless will be one of the factors that determines whether your child will become a statistic as mentioned above or the opposite.

The last, yet most important thing to keep in mind is that this process requires _Healing_. Healing for each party involved: you, your child, and your child's mother. One thing that many parents who struggle to push through the deadbeat zone fail to realize is that this healing takes time, effort, and for you in particular, it will take a lot of endurance which is one of the most important characteristics you must have when making this transition. After all, if you have been absent from your child's life, their perception of you is likely not very optimistic. If you _chose_ to miss out on their life, it's to be expected that your child and his or her mother both carry many ill feelings that will take time to heal. Additionally, they both, along with any other loved ones, will lack trust in you. Trust is something that must be earned, especially if it's lost due to your own actions. In order to gain trust, you must demonstrate your worthiness of it through your actions; show and prove.

Unfortunately, the same is true even in circumstances where your child was alienated from you against your will, because it's probable that your child's perception was tainted by his or her mother. Whatever the case may be, it's important that you understand that your child is in a vulnerable state, and is likely experiencing confusion, hurt, and many other feelings. So, while you may be hurt by what has transpired, you must remember your child's feelings of hurt that are just as valid, and work hard to get to a position where you can make things right for him or her. The only way to accomplish this is by pushing through the deadbeat zone, because once you're out, you will be able to develop a relationship with your child like never before. You will be able to teach him or her many things they need in order to thrive and be successful in life; things a child can only learn from his or her father. Some of those lessons will come from your personal mistakes; others will simply come from wisdom. Either way, these will be things only you will be able to give your child, and both of your lives will change for the better.

Here are a few things to consider when attempting to establish or re-establish a relationship with your child after extensive absence or alienation:

Reunification counseling – If you have been absent for a significant period of time and had no contact or very minimal contact with your child , there will likely be a lot of emotional issues that need to be addressed for the reunification to be successful. For this reason, you should request reunification counseling for you and your child. Qualified Marriage and family therapists and other counselors offer counseling and other support services that lessen or otherwise resolve the upset and uncertainty that comes with the territory of having an absent father.

Supervised visits- Both your child and/or their mother may be uncomfortable with your child visiting with you alone after long stretches of absence. When this is the case, supervised visits (requiring the presence of either a professional monitor, counselor, or trusted family member during visitation) is a good idea, at least at first. Although you may think having a visitation monitor is unnecessary and though it may be uncomfortable for you, it will put your child and/or their mother at ease, while also allowing you to spend quality time with them. Being open to starting with this type of visitation arrangement will show that you're committed to reunifying with your child and will do whatever it takes to make the process less nerve-wracking for them. It's important to create an arrangement that feels like a safe space for everyone involved; this is a good way to start.

Step-up visitation plan- Depending on the circumstances, when children haven't seen their father in a long time, they may hit it off right after commencing or resuming their contact, or it may take a while. Until you see how things go, it's good to start things off slow to avoid unnecessary overwhelm. A step-up plan is essentially a visitation plan that builds up as time goes on. For example, you may start with 3 supervised visits and then graduate to 1 unsupervised full day visit, and then move up to multiple unsupervised daytime visits, and eventually progress to an overnight visit, and hopefully routine overnight weekends, etc. How long each phase takes will really depend on your child and how he or she adjusts to you; it could take weeks, months, or years. It's a good idea to put a plan in place, test it to see how things go, and adjust accordingly. Having a slow, but sure transition will again, put your child at ease and allow you all to focus on building your relationship.

❖ Erratic Can Be Just As Bad As Absent.

One of the most common complaints made by mothers of divided families about the child's father is lack of consistency. When it comes to raising children in divided families, consistency is king key. Lack of consistency can be detrimental to the well-being of your child. Consequently, you have no room to be erratic; your child must know that you are reliable and that they can depend on you no matter what.

While most dads love the idea of being a father, some are unbalanced and inconsistent in doing so because they think being a father is optional. In some cases, while the father will do what's specifically requested of him, he won't take initiative to do too much without being prompted. This goes back to those natural parenting habits/trends I talked about in Chapter I. It really boils down to the type of relationship you want to have with your child. Do you just want to be the parent that does the minimum, dropping by as scheduled or as requested by mom, similar to that of a babysitter? Or do you want to be known as the father who's just as active and involved as mom, building an unbreakable bond with your child?

Because naturally so many presumptions are made that the parental responsibilities belong to the child's mother, as a father of a divided family, you must take action to change this presumption. To do so, you must establish and maintain a level parenting Partnership, by discarding old negative habits. Parenting solely at your convenience rather than full-time is not an option. If you want to be considered equally responsible for your child, you must take initiative rather than waiting on your child's mother to give you certain responsibilities. When making plans for your day, week, month, year, and life, you must do so with your child in mind, not allowing other outside factors to interfere with your priority to parent. Don't think of your parenting time with your child as "your time," and stop at that. Make an effort to be involved in other aspects of your child's life that don't necessarily occur during your parenting time. Attend school events and meetings, participate in extracurricular activities, and take advantage of any additional time you have the opportunity to spend with your child. In other words, go above and beyond.

Another consideration is any negative childhood experiences that you may have had with your parents. If one of your parents may not have been present in your life as much as he/she should have, that doesn't mean that you shouldn't be consistently present for your child. If parenting patterns that you witnessed as a child were unpredictable, that doesn't mean that you should allow your own parenting habits to shift like the wind. Don't settle for mediocrity when you have the potential to be extraordinary. Think about what characteristics, in a perfect world, would've made the perfect father during your childhood and strive to be even better than that. Whatever you do, work hard to be the opposite of erratic, for erratic can be just as bad as being absent.

New Budget

With a child comes new expenses. When the parents of that child live separately, these expenses are even greater, as there are two separate households that must be maintained financially. Consequently, child support becomes an issue that must be addressed. Child support is just one of the things that many divided families are faced with, but few understand. After all, it can be confusing underneath all of the legal terminology, formulas used to calculate support, rules, and exceptions to the rules. As a father, I'm sure one of your main concerns is child support. Specifically, how much you will have to pay and why obtaining support is one of your child's mom's top priorities. Although the fine points of support are much too complex to fully explain in this book, here are the need to know basics:

If obtaining child support seems to be your child's mother's main focus, don't worry, you are not alone. One of the many common complaints fathers make is that their child's mother seems more focused on getting child support than co-parenting or ensuring that the best interests of the child that aren't related to money are fulfilled. If this sounds familiar, there are a few things you should understand. First and foremost, before you get all wound up about child support, understand that asking for child support is a legal right for both you and your child's mother.

❖ Child Support Basics

Both parents have a duty to support their child until they turn 18 years old.

One of the most common misconceptions is that dads are <u>always</u> the parent that will have to pay child support. When a child is born, both parents have a legal duty to support that child until the child is 18 years old. Child support is not based on the gender of the parents. Both moms and dads can be ordered to pay child support.

How support is calculated.

Although both moms and dads can be ordered to pay child support, in many (not all) cases, the father is the parent that is ordered to pay. But, this is not because of his gender. Rather, it is because of the way child support is calculated. Generally, each state has a formula that is used to calculate child support according to that particular state's guidelines. This formula usually calculates the income of the parents, certain expenses, and the amount of time each parent spends with the child to determine who will pay support and the support amount. In situations where the mother has a higher income and/or a lower timeshare (the amount of time spent with their child), the mother may be ordered to pay support. However, oftentimes, fathers have a higher income than mothers. Additionally, more often than not, fathers have a lower timeshare than mothers. Consequently, fathers are commonly the child support payer.

Child support is set up this way in order to ensure that the parent who assumes the most responsibility for the child will have enough financial means to adequately provide for the child. When you think about it, this approach is very logical. After all, the parent who has primary custody of the child will incur day to day expenses that the noncustodial parent will not incur. Specifically, the child needs daily food, clothing and shelter. Additionally, the custodial parent will incur educational, child-care, uninsured medical, and extra-curricular related expenses; not to mention travel expenses related to the same. Considering this, think about your particular situation:

Is your child's mother the primary caretaker of your child? Is she the one who facilitates the daily happenings in your child's life? Is your income higher than hers? If so, you should understand why your support contributions are likely necessary in order to ensure that your child is adequately taken care of.

Many fathers explain that while they don't mind paying child support to take care of their child, they are concerned about whether their child's mother is actually using the child support to provide for the child. Many believe that the mother is in fact using the support for her own personal use. Regardless of whose money is being used for what, the child's needs must be met. So, if your child's mother is spending her own money to take care of your child, but uses your money for her own personal use, the expense is essentially coming from the same source, just in the form of a reimbursement rather than a direct expense. On the other hand, if your child's mother is receiving support from you and not providing for your child (i.e. your child is not being adequately fed, clothed, childcare isn't being paid, etc.) that's a different story. In that case, you should seek legal counsel to assist you with making sure your child support is being used to provide for your child.

If your amount is more than you can afford, or less than you need to receive, you can ask for deductions or adjustments.

Another complaint often made is that the amount of child support ordered is unaffordable. If you are the paying parent, you can request that the court consider special circumstances and make specific deductions to lower your child support amount. If you are the receiving parent and the child support amount is less than you need to support your child, you can ask the court to consider specific circumstances and make adjustments to raise the child support amount. Special circumstances include financial hardship, low income, extraordinary health expenses, a new baby or child support that you pay for a child from a different relationship, etc. The key here is that you must specifically ask the court to consider these things. Otherwise, the court will simply use your basic information into the formula and generate a child support amount based on the state guidelines.

The child support won't change itself.

Regardless of your circumstances, your child support obligation continues until your child turns 18 years old or you or the other party request modification. If your circumstances have changed and justify an increased or decreased amount of child support (i.e. you or the other parent's income, expenses, or time with the child has changed), in order to change your support amount, you must formally request a change from the court. It's important to request modification as soon as possible after you determine that you need the child support amount changed.

If you don't pay your support

After a formal support order is established, if you don't pay as ordered, the consequences can be detrimental. Below is a list of just **some** of the consequences that may come into play if you don't pay child support:

1. Monetary penalties added to support owed.

Failure to pay support can result in owing even more support. Interest and/or penalties vary from state to state. Some states charge interest as high as 12%! Additionally, some states apply penalties. For example, in California, if you are behind on your support more than 30 days, you can incur a penalty of 6 percent of the amount owed, **for each month that it remains unpaid**, up to 72 percent of the amount due!

2. Negative reports to credit bureaus.

If you don't pay child support, the child support agency can report each late or non-payment to the three major credit bureaus. This can have the same impact on your credit rating as not paying your credit cards or mortgage on time.

3. Bank Levies:

Got money in the bank? Direct deposit? Banking institutions report all of the assets they hold. If you don't pay child support, bank levies can be placed on your accounts. If a levy is placed on your account, the money can be taken before you even know it's there. Imagine expecting a paycheck for $3,000, only to find that only $500 is in your account when you get there.

4. Denial of passport

If you owe more than $2,500 in back child support and think you're going on your first vacation out of the country, think again! The U.S. will not issue or renew your passport until your child support is brought current.

5. Seizure of assets.

Not only are your bank accounts at risk, any royalty

checks, dividends, rental incomes, commissions, etc. you're expecting can be seized also. Your real property (i.e. your home or other property you own), cash, your car or other vehicles, and even your safe deposit box contents are also at risk of seizure if you don't pay child support. Nothing is off-limits; your unemployment, disability, or worker's compensation checks and even lottery winnings are at risk of seizure if you don't pay child support.

6. Property Liens.

Liens can also be placed on property you have or intend to sell. If this happens, if/when the property is sold, your owed child support can be taken out of the sale proceeds.

7. License Suspension.

If you don't pay child support, any of your state-issued licenses can be suspended or withheld until you pay the support owed. Most states have a system in place that detects whether one who owes child support has or is applying for a business, professional, and/or driver's license. Yes, that means that if you have or are seeking a license related to your career (doctor, teacher, lawyer, cosmetology, etc.), you may lose or be denied this license until you pay your past due support.

8. Contempt

The consequences worsen if the court finds that you are able to pay support but willfully choose not to. If this happens, you may be held in contempt of court. Contempt actions can be criminal in nature; this means that you could be sentenced to jail time if you fail to pay child support.

Clearly, not paying child support could put you in a devastating position. You could lose everything you have or worse- go to jail. Clearly, if that happens, co-parenting will be the least of your worries, so, if for some reason you are unable to pay child support, you must take action to inform the court of this and request a change. Otherwise, your problems will have a domino effect. Be proactive!

New schedule

An important aspect of co-parenting is establishing a schedule that will allow your child to spend time with you and his or her mother. It is an established fact that it's in a child's best interest that he or she has frequent and continuing contact with both parents (absent extreme circumstances like abuse, neglect, etc.). Although you may be accustomed to taking things day by day, without any structured schedule, unless you and your child's mother have a very good relationship and understanding, co-parenting day by day is *not* a good idea. Just as you and your family have a work schedule, school schedule, sports schedule, and extra-curricular activity schedule, it's important that you also establish a *parenting schedule* and then make adjustments to it day to day as necessary. Hopefully, you and your child's mother can do this between the two of you rather than having a family court decide. This may be hard to accomplish at first, but it is possible and can make all the difference in whether you will have a successful co-parenting experience or a grueling one.

To start, you will need to consider both of your schedules and your child's schedule (including school, tutoring, sports, extra-curricular activities, church, etc.) and determine who will be responsible for your child on which dates and times. You will need to consider holidays, birthdays, spring and summer breaks, vacations, etc. You should also discuss other things that are of importance to you such as communication with the child while he or she is with the other parent, what happens if one of you are unable to have the child on your agreed upon day, where your custody exchanges will take place, what happens if a parent is late, the method of communication between the two of you (i.e., email, text message, phone calls, a co-parent journal, etc.).

New Home Life

Making a transition into that of a divided family is especially difficult if you, your child, and his or her mother previously lived together in the same home. First, you are faced with the task of figuring out if either of you will remain in your current home. If you decide to move out of the home, you are faced with the task of finding a new place to live. Even if one of you decide to stay in the home, the transition isn't necessarily easy because you then have to adjust to your new home environment which previously consisted of two parents, but now only has one. Regardless, the transition is exactly that - a transition - and in order to make the process as smooth as possible, it is important that you maintain as much consistency as possible for the sake of your child.

If you move to a new home, try not to change your child's school districts/schools unless absolutely necessary. At minimum, you should allow your child to continue established relationships with friends that remain in the area. Maintain as many of the same routines that were in place prior to the division and do not disrupt their extra-curricular activities by suddenly switching them to different teams, organizations, or clubs; the division of your family is enough change for now. The key here is not to avoid change, but to minimize additional and unnecessary change until your child has adjusted to this new, divided family situation. So many people make the mistake of deciding to completely uproot their lives because they need to "get away" so they can "start over."

Parents dealing with separation and their own feelings associated with the break-up oftentimes overlook how this affects their children. While family is obviously important to a child, so is his or her familiar social life. Making sudden moves in the midst of an already difficult transition can potentially be traumatizing for your child. Consider more than just your own feelings and think about how this will affect your child. While some children adjust quickly without issue, others must be guided through this process delicately. Remember, this is not their fault. Your child should not have to suffer simply because you and his or her mother's relationship did not work out.

Blending Your Family

❖ *The New Guy*

Out of all of the new things a divided family must adjust to, most parents report the most difficult being the adjustment to new people in their child's life, specifically the mom's - new guy. To a certain extent this is understandable. After all, this is your child we are talking about here and it's your duty as his or her father to look out for his or her best interest. Considering the fact that this new guy is the equivalent of a stranger, reluctance is not unreasonable. I get it. I have three children and just the thought of the wrong person entering into their lives makes me very uncomfortable. Besides, in this world we're living in, people are crazy! However, the reality is that since you and your child's mother aren't together, it's going to happen at some point. Your child is going to meet the new guy (in some cases, they'll meet more than one new guy, but that's a different book) and unfortunately, regardless of whether you approve of him or not, if your child's mother wants him to be involved in your child's life, then he will be; there's nothing you can or should want to do about it unless you have a very <u>good</u> <u>reason</u>. And no, "I don't want my child around another dude" is not a good reason. So unless you have a real good reason (i.e., he mistreats your child, is dangerous, literally crazy, etc.) it's time to step out of the boy zone and into the grown man zone.

EVALUATE _YOUR_ ACTIONS:

- *Do you refuse to accept your child's mother's new man and refuse to facilitate a relationship between him and your child?*

- *Do you insist that your child not be around the new man?*

- *If you don't want your child around the new man, what is your reason? Is it simply because you don't know him? Because he's not you?*

ACTION STEP:

If you answered "yes" to any of these questions, your next action step is to face the fact that he is now going to be a part of your child's life and unless you can show that he is unfit to be around your child, there is nothing you can do about it.

Her Lover = Your Friend

How you handle the new man will largely depend on whether you have the immature mindset of a boy, or the mature mindset of a man. A mature man, regardless of how he feels about his child's mother moving on, will do what is necessary to make the best of the situation; in this case, ensuring that if another man is going to be around his child, that the man and his child have the best relationship possible without interference caused by him. Although initially, it's natural to be apprehensive about another man stepping into a parent-like role for your child, once you've properly dealt with the division between you and your child's mother and any ill feelings you had toward her, you will be able to think and act maturely, making sure the sole focus is the best interest of your child regardless of what happened between you and their mother and regardless of who is new in the picture. Believe it or not, the role this new man plays in your child's life largely depends on your rapport with the new man.

When you or your child's mother start seriously dating someone who will essentially be involved in your child's life, at that point your divided family becomes a *blended* family. This is especially true if either of you marry that person, which will technically make that person your child's step-parent. Even if neither of you actually get married, as long as there is another man or woman in the picture, the general principle is the same. It's important that you set aside any ill feelings you have toward your child's mother or the new man so that all of you can come to a mutual understanding. This goes back to the concept of parenting as an equal parenting Partner and *managing* the situation.

Why is your rapport with the new man so important? Because, if this man is going to be around your child, it's important that you eliminate any negative vibes between the two of you as much as possible. The better your rapport with him, the better his relationship with your child and theoretically, the better he will treat your child. The better he treats your child, the less drama you will have in your life, and the greater the chances you will have peace in your divided, now blended family. Additionally, you can't forget that this person will have a substantial impact on the type of life your child lives and the type of person they become. So, with this in mind, it will behoove you to build a positive bond with this man for the sake of your child. So how do you do this? Well, it's actually quite simple, through communication and by establishing boundaries. As I have stated several times before, communication is key in divided families! Some boundaries will come naturally, others you will have to directly address and discuss. The first thing you need to consider is the fact that he is new to your family. He doesn't know you and you don't know him. He doesn't know if you are a "crazy baby daddy" or a level-headed, mature father. He doesn't know how you feel about a new man being in the picture or how your child will respond to his presence.

SIDE NOTE: *Are you the "crazy baby daddy?"* While I addressed the "crazy baby mama," I didn't touch on the "crazy baby daddy." Yes! They exist too. It's time to get real. Before we go any further, it's very important for you to evaluate your actions. Do you act like the "crazy" one? Are you extremely unreasonable when it comes to co-parenting? Do you constantly put your own interests before the interests of your child? Now that we have established that you are the new parenting Partner of your divided/blended family, responsible for protecting a "2 billion dollar business deal," take a look at your behavior and determine if it is reasonable. Would your behavior jeopardize that deal? The best way to understand how your actions affect others is to put yourself in that person's shoes. Be honest, logical and reasonable. Then answer the question, how would you react to "whatever" it is that you have done or said. If your reaction would be positive, then you've taken the correct approach. If your reaction would be negative or you would feel offended, then you've taken the incorrect approach. DO NOT be the "crazy baby daddy." Remember, you are the parenting Partner. You are held to a higher standard and you have an image to set and maintain......

Back to the point: Although he may not show it, he may actually be apprehensive coming into the situation because he doesn't know what to expect, and he won't know until you talk to him. A great way to break the ice with the new man is to try to minimize the apprehension he may be experiencing. Try to put him at ease and let him know that you are a grown man whose only concern is that of your child. Let him know that you will not participate in or tolerate drama. Get to know him when he comes around. Ask about his family, where he grew up, about his career, etc. I'm not saying you have to be his best friend, but you should want to know who this person is that's going to be spending a significant amount of time around your child and to be cordial with him.

Now, before you get your pen and paper and start writing your 20 questions, let me be clear, I'm not telling you to give him a pop quiz or drill him as if he's being interviewed. At this point an interview isn't necessary, as he already has the position of being a part of your child's life. Now that he's in this position, your goal is to figure out the best way to make his position work best for your family. Figure out his strengths and weaknesses and what he brings to the table. Spark a conversation with him similar to one that you would start with someone who you were introduced to by one of your close friends. The key is to be genuine. You need to show genuine interest in getting to know him and you actually should be interested! After all, this person could ultimately have strong influence on your child one day so you should be on the same page, or at least in the same book.

One sure way to put the new man at ease is to ensure him that you no longer have a romantic interest in your child's mom, nor do you have a desire to control her actions. As we all know, men can be territorial when it comes to their woman. You can establish this by your actions, without ever having to speak on the subject. Just treat your child's mom with respect and respect the fact that there is a new man in her life. Offer to involve him in your child's activities if he has a genuine interest in being involved. This will not only give you an opportunity to see how he interacts with your child, but will also give you the opportunity to personally observe his personality as opposed to simply taking his word. Including him in your child's activities will also put your child at ease; he or she will be able to see the positive relationship and understand that it's okay for them to have the same positive relationship. On the other hand, this will also encourage your child to open up to you about this person, specifically if he or she has some reservations about him. The more your child sees that you are interested in building this rapport with the new man, the more likely he or she will reveal whether they want that to happen. Whatever you do, under no circumstances should you reveal your ill feelings you have about the new man to your child (with the exception of genuine safety concerns). This only leads to drama, confuses your child, and makes your child more uncomfortable than he or she may already be.

So what about those common cases where you would ideally like to build a positive relationship with the new man, but he is in fact the problem? What if he, refuses to build a rapport with you, but would rather have an ego battle and overall just create a negative situation? Well, you have to think of him as an extension of your child's mother and handle him the same way you would if she behaved in this manner (as discussed in Chapters I. and II.); lead by example and fight that fire with fire only if necessary. Remember, people cannot keep up drama with themselves, if they can that's when it's likely that they are crazy and need to seek professional help. The more reasonable you are, the more reasonable he will likely be or eventually become. Although it may seem like *eventually* will never come, at some point, something has to give. Just continue to do the right thing, put your child's best interest first, and things will fall into place; if they don't you can easily take the *proper* steps necessary to get resolutions. Remember, you are the parenting Partner, therefore you must handle things professionally, appropriately, and as necessary.

❖ *Your New Lady*

So let's talk about your new lady or your future new lady. Your child's mother isn't the only one who will bring someone new into the picture. You have a life too right? So at some point while you are establishing this new life, you will meet someone that you may be interested in. However, dating as a father of a divided family is completely different than dating as a single man with no children. As a man with no children, you would date solely for yourself, for the fun of it, and sometimes maybe even with little to no regard to the future of your relationship with the new lady, as you may not necessarily intend to have a serious relationship with her. Quite the opposite, when you are a father; you have a responsibility to your child to date more carefully, with your child's interests in mind.

Even if your child's mother continues to be actively involved in your child's life, it is still important to understand that any woman you bring into your child's life will play a significant role. Children watch and learn from everyone around them. For this reason, you must be very careful about who you allow to become an influence in your child's life. It's also important to remember that children need stability and consistency as much as possible. Your child's stability is already a little shaky because he or she now has two separate households; and his or her parents aren't together not to mention the other new factors as previously mentioned. So, when bringing new people into your child's life, it is important to be very mindful of what your child is already dealing with in order to minimize disorder. Specifically, take note of the following three very important points:

1) Every Woman You Date Does Not Need to Meet Your Child

Prior to settling down with someone, you may go on several dates, have several flings (if that's your style), etc. Although many of these prospective mates may be good gals, that does not mean they should meet your child right

91

away. Now when I say "meet," I don't mean if you happen to run into her while you and your child are out and about, turn the other way and take cover. I mean "meet" as in the lady becoming involved in your child's life. Unfortunately, children do not understand the dating process. When they meet someone new, they will likely expect that person to become part of their life. That's great if you and the new gal hit it off and she takes on that role. But what if soon after your child meets her, you realize you are not feeling her? What if she turns out to be simply a thing of the moment? Although this may not be a big deal for most adults, this is huge for children! Especially if they have gotten to know this new woman, look for her, and expect her to be around. In this situation, what results is a child who is now not only forced to adjust to a divided family, but also having to adjust to the new woman who has come and gone. If this happens more than once, you are now creating a cycle of people coming in and out of your child's life, which could ultimately influence his or her interaction with people in the future throughout his or her life; hence they may grow up and think this inconsistency is normal. This can be detrimental to your child.

There are many people, both men and women, who grew up in environments where nothing was consistent, especially their relationships with those around them. This creates distrust and hinders their ability to build and maintain significant relationships with others. This vicious cycle is one that may or may not be broken depending on whether they get the professional help they need. You, however, can help prevent this cycle by simply being a little more careful about who you introduce into your child's life. Although there is no specific time limit which determines how long you should date the new woman before you introduce her to your child, a good rule of thumb is that in order to meet your child, you and that person should be at the point where you are ready to take your dating relationship to the next level. Now, I'm not saying you have to "put a ring on it" before she can meet your child. But, you should wait until the two of you decide to be in a committed relationship (i.e. "boyfriend/girlfriend") and that person must also be committed to accepting your child and plan to be there for the long haul as a parental figure. Of course this rule of thumb is not fool-proof, as things don't always work out as you expect, but it will potentially lessen the chances of unnecessary introductions and disappearances.

2) The New Woman is Not Your "Friend" or Your Child's "Aunt"

If I hear of one more confused child referring to their dad's girlfriend as daddy's "friend" or "aunt so and so" I think I'm going to scream! Referring to a lady you're dating as your "friend" may sound like a good idea, but it's not! Calling her your "friend" does nothing but confuse your child, specifically by giving them a false perception of what a friend is. First of all, relationships with friends are platonic. Anything outside of that takes your relationship outside of the "friendship" zone. Next, in true friendships, *most* friendships last. Before classifying the lady you are dating as a "friend," ask yourself: "If for some reason this doesn't work out between us, will she still be a part of my child's and my life?" If you can honestly answer this question "yes," then fine, refer to her as your friend. But, if your answer is "no" or even "I don't know," she's *not* your "friend", she is a lady you are dating. Remember, your child does not need any added confusion or inconsistency in his or her life. Creating this perception that "friends" come and go is contributing to the creation of the in and out cycle previously discussed and is not in your child's best interest.

The same principle applies to having your child call the woman you are dating his or her "aunt"...what!? This is not your sister (is it?). Nor is this your close friend that you consider the sister you never had! Stop it! Again, this is just confusing your child. *(Side note: I'm very saddened by the fact that I have to discuss this, but I have seen and heard enough)*. Since when did it become okay to date your sister?... Never! And I would hope that you do not want to lead your child to believe this. She's not your sister, she's not your child's aunt so please, do not refer to her as such.

3) You and Your New Lady Must Know and Understand
Her Role and Boundaries

The new woman's role is not to be your child's mom. However, she should be ready, willing, and able to assume a positive role in your child's life based on the relationship that she has with you. Is this a parental-like role? Yes, naturally it will be, but it's not a replacement role. She must understand and respect the fact that your child has a mother, and act accordingly. Under no circumstances should you direct your child to refer to the new woman as "mom," "mommy" or any variation of that title; this is the ultimate sign of disrespect to his or her mother and can cause a lot of major problems. You tell me, do you want your child calling the new man "daddy?" I'm guessing not.

You must consider that just as you may be uneasy about new men coming into your child's life, so is your

95

child's mother. So what do you do? The best approach to take when bringing a new woman into your divided family is to show your child's mother the same respect that you would like her to show you. I know I may sound repetitive when I say, "Lead by example," but doing so facilitates the greatest potential for a positive relationship with your child's mother. Consider how this new woman coming into the picture would make your child's mother feel and try to minimize the reluctance she may have for this change by being respectful to the relationship that your child's mom has with your child and that once existed between the two of you.

Prior to introducing your new woman to your child, talk to your child's mother about it. Let her know that you have been dating someone and that you are now at a serious place in your relationship which includes introducing her to your child. Explain that out of respect for her and in consideration of your child's feelings and understanding, you wanted to wait until you knew this person was in it for the long haul and wasn't just a thing for the moment. Ask her if she would like to meet the new woman first, before you introduce her to your child. She may say yes or she may decline, but by putting the ball in her court and giving her the option, she will see both that you are consciously making an effort to co-parent with her and keep her informed and involved in major decisions that will essentially affect your child. She may not like the fact that you're moving on, but at least she can't say that she was blind-sided and her child suddenly had a new stepmom that she had no idea about. I know this seems like a lot, but it's a very important part of the business of co-parenting.

Even if your child's mother did not show you this same courtesy I am suggesting, remember, always lead by example. Show her the right way to co-parent and hopefully she will eventually follow. One of the key characteristics of a good co-parent is the ability to be the bigger person no matter what the other parent does. Do not expect her to lead your divided family in the direction that it should go, as that may be unrealistic at this time. You may have to step up and be proactive! You want to neutralize as many potentially negative situations as possible. By communicating your intentions to your child's mother beforehand, you are starting off your new relationship on a more positive note than you would if you were to all of a sudden have some new woman around your child without notice and your child's mother found out from a third party, or worse - your child. This also reassures your child's mother that you are not trying to replace her role as your child's mother and may even encourage her to take the lead in getting to know your new woman and incorporating her into your divided/blended family.

IV.

THE LEGAL WAY

Apart from your divided family situation, in order to protect your family from unnecessary interruptions and prevent unnecessary problems, the most important thing you need to do is take certain legal actions.

One of the most beneficial things you can do for your divided family is establish child custody orders. Formal custody orders make divided/blended family life a little less complicated. Not only will it create a legal record as to who has the authority to make decisions related to your child, but it will also outline who your child will live with, what the other parent's visitation will be (if any), and much more. Many families make the mistake of skipping this step because they don't realize the consequences of not having orders. It's important to know that despite what you may believe is the best custody/visitation arrangement for your children, unless you and the other parent agree on these arrangements, custody is not automatic.

A Father's Rights

If you *insist* on your father's rights, you will have them (absent extreme circumstances that prove you should not). While it is true that often mothers are granted custody, if a father wants custody, he can be granted custody as well. I see it happen every day, I help fathers do this every day, so never assume that just because she's "mom", that you have no chance of getting custody or even reasonable visitation with your child.

When a child's parents are unmarried, unless a court action already exists related to custody/guardianship of your child, parents "technically" don't have any legal/enforceable rights to that child. In order to establish these rights, a court action establishing parentage must be filed- this must be done even if the parents both signed the child's birth certificate or voluntary declaration of paternity. This often becomes problematic for fathers in particular, because unlike mothers, paternity isn't absolute (i.e. mothers can dispute paternity of a father, but because mothers carry and give birth to their children, fathers likely have no grounds to dispute maternity). For this reason, it's important for parents to establish parentage as soon as possible after a child is born.

Even when a child's parents are married, custody is still not simple. When parents separate or divorce, neither parent is any more entitled to custody of the children than the other until the court makes orders. Because custody is essentially a "free for all" before the court makes orders (either parent may keep the children with them, pick them up from school, etc.) many families end up fighting over the kids unnecessarily, causing disruption in daily routines and preventing stability for the children involved. For this reason, it's important to request specific custody orders simultaneously when filing for divorce or as soon as possible thereafter.

By establishing custody early on, your child's status quo is documented for the record in case there is a custody dispute later. There will be no question as to who has rights to your child and any violations of those rights are easily enforceable.

Here's why I'm telling you all of this. I want you to understand that regardless of what your child's mother may say or do, you have a place in your child's life just as much as she does. Don't let anyone tell you otherwise. Yes, you may have to put in a little extra work or effort to establish that place, but it's still your place…if you want it that is.

A lot of fathers complain that they shouldn't have to go through extra steps to assume an equal parenting role. While this may be true, the reality is that you'll spend more time and money fighting to avoid the extra steps than you would to just take the extra steps to establish your rights. Think about it like this: Moms also have an "extra step". They have to go through the "extra step" of carrying the child and giving birth. The only "extra step" you have to do is sign, fill out, and file paperwork acknowledging that you are and are willing to be a dad for your children. And, if you do this, you are essentially requiring the mom to answer and creating a presumption that it may be in the best interest of your child to live with you and/or have a relationship with you; once this is done, the court will be required to consider it.

Steps To Establish Custody Orders

Thanks to television and media, many families think that the only way to establish custody orders is to "go to court." Going to court is one way for you to establish custody orders, but in many cases it's unnecessary.

Letting a judge decide the fate of your divided/blended family rarely fares well for anyone involved. Although on television, the court process is often portrayed as being easy breezy, in reality, it's much more complex. When representing clients, I try my best to avoid the courtroom as much as possible. In my opinion, this should be a last resort.

FAQ: If my child's mother and I agree to work together regarding custody do I still need custody orders?

If your child's mother is present, custody orders will establish stability and parenting guidelines that will help minimize future confusion. When parents are civil enough to cooperate, they assume they can just "work it out" between themselves without the need for any formal arrangements such as a custody order or written parenting plan.

My answer to this question is almost always, you don't have to, but you should.

I know you may think that formalizing your agreement is an unnecessary step, and, there is a very slim chance that you are right. Yes, the idea of working together, taking things day by day, and caring for the kids according to what's going on with your family's daily schedule is a great idea. But, more often than not, these informal arrangements become problematic. This is especially true when the parents first separate or before they have consciously established a positive co-parenting relationship. If you fail to formalize your agreement, you are very possibly setting yourself up for unnecessary chaos.

If you and your child's mother get along well, great! However, it is to be expected that you will not always get along and you definitely will not agree on everything. Heck, if you did agree on everything you would probably still be together, right? In divided/blended families, at some point, parents typically will likely have a disagreement regarding the children's schedule, activities, childcare, financial needs, discipline, or other issues; if there is no set remedy in place, that's when the drama begins. When this happens, one parent will refuse to cooperate, refuse:

- to "allow" the kids to go with the other parent,

- to contribute to a financial obligation,

- to confer with the other parent regarding an important decision related to the kids,

The list goes on and on of the problems that can potentially arise when informal arrangements go sour.

The safest approach to protect your family is to be proactive, understanding the potential for problems and disagreements, and plan accordingly. Hopefully, you can develop a cooperative co-parenting relationship and live happily ever after, but...you know the saying "prepare for the worst, hope for the best" That is especially true here. The best way to prepare for the worst is to establish a formal parenting plan. Essentially, this means you want to establish a parenting plan and then have it signed by a judge so that it becomes an enforceable court order, albeit one that YOU create, it will still be enforceable in the event that you or the other parent wake up one day or randomly have a change of heart and decide that you aren't going to follow the agreement.

Remember, co-parenting is a business and the only asset of your business is your child. Your job is to take preventative steps that are necessary to protect your child. All successful businesses have written agreements that govern their business relationships; those that do not are usually the ones that do not take their business seriously and have the most legal problems in the long run. Similarly, co-parents who do not have formalized agreements are the ones who generally end up seeking emergency court orders and/or fighting in ugly custody battles. The purpose of formalizing your parenting schedule is to protect you and your children from unnecessary spontaneous disputes, thereby maintaining peace.

The idea is that by formalizing your agreement you will both be held accountable for your actions. You will have more of an incentive to follow the agreement, because you will know that failure to do so can result in criminal penalties. Additionally, you will feel secure in knowing that in the event that the other parent does violate the order, you have the option to seek enforcement from the police or court system if absolutely necessary. I have lost count of the number of situations that I have handled that included complaints of their child being "kidnapped" by the other parent. The most common situations are those where the parents have been alternating custody of their child on their own, without a court order.

Keep in mind, circumstances surrounding your family will change constantly and you may need to deviate from your written parenting plan accordingly. You will always have the option to agree to change things day by day if necessary. But, once your plan is signed by the court, even if you never have to take action to enforce it, your family will have the security in knowing that there are rules, schedules, and guidelines in place that are best for your family, irrespective of how you may be feeling about each other in a particular moment, that must be followed to maintain stability and consistency for your children. If your child's mother is present, formal orders will provide specific guidelines and minimize confusion. If your child's mother is erratic, custody orders can curtail her ability to just "parent at her convenience" because there will be set visitation dates and times that will be designated as her "parenting time." If your child's mother is absent or a deadbeat, custody orders that identify you as the parent with sole legal and physical custody will ensure that there is no misunderstanding regarding who has custody and control of your child in the event that your child's mother suddenly decides to show up unexpectedly demanding immediate access to your child. Having an established order will also decrease the difficulty in challenging any claims that you are keeping your child from their mother, interfering with her parental rights, or other similar allegations. Hopefully you've already secured custody and visitation orders for your children. Nonetheless, it's better late than never, so if you have not, now is a good time to prepare to do so.

❖ *Mediation*

If you and your child's mother are not yet to a point of accord and able to reach an agreement on your own, or if you simply want a professional to facilitate discussion between you two, mediation may be an ideal solution for you rather than jumping to litigation. Because my law practice also includes mediation, I'm able to compare the results of both processes. Although I'm successful achieving favorable results for my clients through litigation (the court trial process) mediation is a far more beneficial option in my opinion. I think mediation is the best way to get the best custody orders for your family because you are able to work with a professional who can help you make knowledgeable decisions, while also working with your co-parent to make sure that those decisions are best for your family.

Mediation is one of the most practical ways for parents to resolve disputes related to child custody, time-sharing, visitation, child support, and co-parenting. As no divided family is the same, no two mediators are the same and no two mediation sessions will be the same. However, typically, mediation takes place in a relaxed, yet structured atmosphere. Parents meet with the mediator to facilitate an open discussion during which they are able to confidentially communicate and discuss any issues of concern, goals, and proposed solutions.

The mediator is a neutral party. Through my mediation process, although I do not represent either party, I work carefully with both parents to help them figure out what will work best for *their* divided/blended family. I will then specifically tailor a unique agreement for the parents, which will ultimately be submitted to the Court with a request that it be made an enforceable court order.

❖ *Formal Request for Orders*

Unfortunately, not all parents will be able to reach an agreement regarding custody/visitation of their children. The last resort, if you and your child's mother have been unable to agree on issues related to your child, may be to file a motion or other request for the court to make specific orders related to the custody and support of your child. When you hear people say "I'll see you in court," this is the process they are referencing. This is the least preferred method of handling things the legal way because it can be very risky and daunting for many reasons:

<u>Family Court Child Custody proceedings are lengthy.</u>
Compared to mediation, which is typically completed in a few sessions, family law litigation is a much lengthier process. Although temporary orders may be issued shortly after your case begins, getting permanent orders takes time – in some cases, a very long time. Exactly how long depends on you, the other parent, any lawyers that are involved, and how much conflict exists.

<u>When you litigate, no one "wins."</u> There is no such thing as really "winning" in a litigated custody case. Asking the court to make decisions related to your family is risky because you will likely not get 100% of what you want. To get just 1/2 of what you want will likely cost you a lot of time and money required to build the case.

<u>Legal Battles are Expensive</u> even if you don't hire a lawyer to represent you, you may quickly find out that there is no "cheap" way to litigate a case. Filing fees, service of process charges, court reporters, professional evaluations, and more can easily lead to thousands of dollars in costs. And once lawyers get involved on either side, that amount can easily triple.

<u>Judges don't know you.</u> When you litigate your case, you're essentially putting your family's life into the hands of a stranger. They don't know anything about you, your child's other parent, or your children. Their decision is solely based on what is presented to them as evidence. Quite frankly, we all know that evidence presented to the court is not always the best reflection of the true circumstances or complete facts (especially if you don't have a lawyer).

<u>The best interest of your child.</u> The court is going to make a determination based on what it feels is in the "best interest" of YOUR child (who they know nothing about and may never meet). Your definition of "best interest" and the court's idea of best interest may be on two different spectrums. The court will consider many different factors including, but not limited to:

- The child's existing living arrangements, schedule, and any potential effects significant change to such arrangements will have on the child.

- The parents' relationships with the child.

- The parents' lifestyles including abhorrent and

criminal behavior or allegations of such.

- The health of the parents (both physical and mental).

- The living situation of the parents and their ability to provide for the child.

- The parents' attitudes towards the other parent's rights to the child.

- What the child wants

- The child's age and gender

The court's order may not make any sense for your family, but once it's issued, you have to follow it unless you and the other parent finally can agree to change it. If you and your child's other parent can put your differences aside and really think about what's best for your child, you'll probably be much better off.

Judges are human Granted, they are humans with decision power not afforded to the average layperson, but...the fact still remains that, at the end of the day, they are just like you. They have a life, family, things on their "to do" list, and more. So, although it's easy to put them on a pedestal, just like you they make mistakes, have bad days, get frustrated, don't understand, and are at work. Don't walk into the courthouse expecting to appear before a supernatural human that can work magic…you'll be disappointed.

<u>Agreements feel better</u> When you are able to sit down with the other parent and compromise, although you may not get everything you want, you'll at least know that what you're getting will be something that is reasonable based on your family's needs. Agreements open the door to cooperation. It's not something that is forced, but a decision YOU had a hand in. For this reason, once you're able to reach an agreement on the bigger issues, you'll slowly be able to reach an agreement on other things and learn to work together for the benefit of your child.

The fact of the matter is, when you are asking a court to make a decision that affects your life, they will not always get it right. With that in mind, if at all possible, you should avoid getting to the point that the court has to make a decision that could change your family's life (for better or worse) for you.

Parenting Plans:

Regardless of which process used to obtain your formal custody orders, in order for your custody orders to benefit your family, many things must be considered.

There are typically several things that are automatically included. Things such as which parent will have the custody and control of the children during each day, who will be in charge of specific extracurricular activities, where the children will go to school, who the children will be with during the holidays, who the medical providers will be, rules required to change the child's school etc. are generally included in most plans.

However, there are several things that oftentimes go unmentioned that you may want to consider discussing during your negotiations or requesting in your formal requests submitted to the court. While it's impossible to include every single foreseeable important issue in your parenting plan, the point of a parenting plan/custody orders is to ensure that there is little room for misunderstanding, misinterpretation, and that the plan can easily be enforced if the need arises. Just like any other contract, more is better than less. The more specific and clear you are regarding the terms of the agreement, the less confusion and conflict there will likely be. When developing your parenting plan, there are many things to consider, but the most important thing that should guide you in making decisions, is what's best for your children.

Here are a few specifics to consider including in your parenting agreement:

1. Who is responsible for transporting your children to and/or from one parent to the other? Where will custody exchanges take place and at what time? May 3rd parties be present during the exchanges? (If one parent is often in the company of someone who likes to initiate or instigate conflict, you can ask the court for orders specifying who can and cannot be present during exchanges.

2. What happens if one parent has to cancel their time? Do they get makeup time with your child? Or is it just forfeited?

3. What if one parent decides to move? Do they have to provide the address to the other parent? (they should), and how far in advance or after

the move should the new address be provided to the other parent?

4. Child care – who is allowed to babysit your children? Friends? Family? A mutually chosen babysitter? Anyone?

5. Will the children get phone time with the other parent when they aren't with them and vice versa? If so, on what days, how many times? And at what specific time?

6. New significant others – when will they be able to meet your children?

7. Contact with certain people – are there certain people you agree should not have contact with your children?

8. Does either parent have special decision-making authority on certain issues? For example: is one parent in charge of selecting sports teams, extracurricular activities, the school the children will attend, etc.? Or must all of these things be decided jointly. What happens if you can't agree on things requiring joint decision? Is there a neutral party who can act as your "tie-breaker"? Or do you have a "rock-paper-scissors" type of

solution? (Yes, this matters, because otherwise you'll end up in front of a judge over every disagreement.)

9. Who will have your children for which holidays? Where will holiday exchanges take place and at what exact day and time? If you are splitting spring break, are you meeting at 12 noon on the day that marks the halfway mark?

10. What is the remedy if either parent habitually violates the agreement? Do you intend for the agreement to be enforced by law enforcement if necessary? If so, specifically state this in the agreement, as some law enforcement agencies are reluctant to get involved if it's not specified.

11. And of course we can't forget provisions related to expenses – who will be financially responsible for childcare/school tuition? Who will cover the costs of extra-curricular activities? What about medical insurance premiums and uninsured medical expenses, etc.

Although no parenting plan is the same, and all of the above is not necessary for every family, these are just a few of the provisions to consider including in your agreement to avoid confusion and provide clarity, just in case. It's better to have a lot of unnecessary specifics than to not be specific enough, and leave room for mix-up.

The Last Resort

So what happens when you have honestly put in countless effort to develop a peaceful parenting relationship with your child's mother, but your efforts have failed? What if your child's mother still does not cooperate and deliberately violates a court order? Sadly, there will be some moms that no matter what you do to develop a positive relationship with her, she will not cooperate and will do (or won't do) whatever she can in order to make your life miserable. There will always be that one who just doesn't care! She doesn't care about her child, you, or even herself for that matter. The good news is that if you have handled your case the legal way, you will have remedies. Although the process that comes with resorting to these remedies is yet again, disruptive and frustrating for you, nonetheless the remedies are available and you are still better off than you would be if you had not handled things the legal way. Once you have a court order in place, you have a few options in the event that your child's mother refuses to follow the court order. Below are the two most commonly used:

❖ *Enforcement*

In the event that your child's mother (or you) violates the court order related to child custody, most law enforcement officers will enforce the order. To do this, you will need to take a certified copy of your court order to the nearest police station and file a report. You may request that an officer enforce the order. If the department is willing to enforce the order, they will go to the location where your child is being withheld and speak to the parent in violation of the order and demand that they turn over the child. If she follows the officer's request, the officer will then bring your child to you. In the event that your child's mother refuses to turn your child over, in some cases the officer will make an arrest, but in most, the officer will usually make a police report so that you may file a court action for enforcement/contempt

❖ *Contempt*

A contempt action may be filed if you or child's mother willfully violates the child custody, child support, or any other court order. Contempt actions are criminal in nature and for the most part are considered misdemeanors, punishable by up to six months in county jail and/or a fine up to $1,000.

These are obviously measures that hopefully you will not be forced to take, but as the parenting Partner of your divided family, it is imperative that you know of your rights and duties as a parent, and be ready and willing to utilize all options available to ensure the welfare and safety of your child.

V.

THE BUSINESS OF

CO-PARENTING

The business of co-parenting is just like any other business; it takes genuine commitment, hard work, and constant, conscious efforts. Although it may require major adjustments in the way you have been dealing with your divided family, once you take full responsibility for your mindset and your actions, and can keep them in check regardless of what your child's mother is doing, you will become the master of you and your child's future and your ability to live in peace.

Just like businesses have bylaws to abide by, so should your blended family. There are several things that if implemented, can prevent, lessen, and even destroy drama in your family. Although all divided/blended families are different, the general co-parenting "business" rules can be applied to all and expanded upon as you see fit.

Co-Parent Business Bylaws

❖ *Blended Family Language*

As divided/blended families, we already face an uphill battle to get to a point that we feel like a solid family unit. The way you speak of your family is just one of the things that impacts the dynamic of your relationship. One of the ways to think about it: when someone's words are encouraging, we feel good. When someone speaks well of us, it makes us happy. The same goes for your family. If you speak of your family as though you are unified, at some point you will likely be. If you speak of your family like you're divided, that's how you'll remain.

❖ *"Baby Mommas and Baby Daddies"*

Naturally, you may refer to your child's mother as your "ex", or worse- your "baby mama." Unless your family is on a drama-filled reality tv show (or unless that's your goal), you should stop referring to your child's mother as your "baby mama."

Believe it or not, we speak our worlds into existence. If all you want is a "baby mama," then carry on referring to her as such. However, if it's your desire to have a positive mother figure in your child's life, you should start speaking that over her. That is your child's mother, your co-parenting partner. You are your child's father. Respect and refer to each other as such.

❖ *"The steps"*

Yes, we know that a "stepfamily" is one in which one or both spouses have children from another relationship.

But, when families blend, why is there a need to distinguish? Everyone in the family knows who the "mom", "dad", and "step"-parents are, there's really no need to remind each other every day. To me, referring to your family as a "step" anything only adds an element of separation. The only time I refer to my stepson as my "stepson" is if I'm providing a detailed explanation that requires it (such as this book). When I introduce him to someone, I refer to him as my son. When I speak of him, I always say "I have three children", not "I have two of my own and one stepchild." We are one family unit, regardless of our bloodline, and there's no reason for us to feel otherwise.

It was no different for my ~~step~~son. Before we decided that "step" was just not a word we would use in our family, I could see the discomfort in his demeanor when he would introduce or refer to me as his "stepmom." Now, he comfortably refers to me as his mom (and clarifies if necessary), bonus mom, or mom #2. This decreases the need for him to provide an explanation about our relationship to those who don't really need it.

If you have to distinguish between your biological and marital relationship, try using "bonus child", "bonus mom", or "bonus dad" instead of "step." Step feels more like a burden or inconvenience, while "bonus" feels more like an advantage, something special, something more solid.

❖ *Disparaging remarks*

Again, the words you speak regarding your divided/blended family are instrumental in the dynamic of your relationships. This includes not only the words you use to refer to your family members, but also the words you use to describe them. The mantra "If you don't have anything nice to say, don't say anything at all" is best applied here.

Disparaging remarks are those words that are derogatory, disapproving, or critical. You know, the ones you may speak (or be tempted to speak) on you and your child's mother's worst day. The words you want to say about her, but you shouldn't say out loud. The words that if your child were to hear them, would make them uncomfortable. Think about it like this: Regardless of how you feel about your child's mother, the fact remains that she is still their mom. She is *your* Ex, but not your child's Ex. Your relationship with her may be over, but her relationship with your child will remain forever. Considering this, it's imperative that you not be the cause of any dysfunction in their relationship. By making negative comments about your child's mother to them, in their presence, or within their hearing distance, you can potentially cause them to feel negatively about their mother. You in essence may be transferring your own personal emotions and opinions to them. The same goes for your friends and family; their negative opinions about your child's mother are off limits in the presence of your children. Children repeat what they hear grown-ups say, they learn what we teach them. What are you teaching them about their mother? Your negative perceptions of her may be correct. However, it's not your job to ruin their independent perception of her. The reality is, if she's really as "bad" as you think, you won't have to say one word to your child about it; he/she will learn everything they need to know about her on their own, based on her actions and interactions with them.

❖ *Check your Village*

Ever heard the quote: "It takes a village to raise a child?" This quote speaks volumes. In order for children to thrive and develop into the wonderful human beings they have the potential to become, they need positive, supportive, influential people in their lives to give them direction and teach them core values of life. The same applies to your co-parenting relationship with your child's mother. In order to get to a place of peace and cooperation with your child's mother, you must be surrounded by people who support this goal. There's nothing worse than someone who has good intentions when it comes to doing something positive, yet is surrounded by naysayers and people with negative attitudes whose energy transfers to them.

I remember there was a lady who followed me on social media and was interested in one of my resources/programs for divided/blended families. She tagged her friend in the comments of one of my promotional posts indicating that she was thinking of participating in my program because she was tired of the drama with her child's father. Rather than supporting her, her "friend" responded in the comments, basically saying "you don't need this, you do just fine being both mom and dad for your child." This was so disappointing to me: here you had a young lady who acknowledged the fact that she was struggling to build a positive relationship with her child's father and was considering getting help to change her situation. Yet, the one friend that she may have called on for sound advice basically told her "you don't need to change anything, your child is just fine without their dad." This is the perfect example of needing to check your village.

Ever heard the saying "show me who your closest friends are and I'll show you your future"? Yet another mantra that applies to divided/blended families. If your circle consists of a bunch of no good, "baby daddies" whose children don't have relationships with them, naturally you may take on the same attitude. However, if you're surrounded by parents who are constantly on a mission to create better for their children, then you will naturally be inspired to strive for the same. It's hard to aim for progress when no one around you is progressing. It's hard to be optimistic about your partnership with your child's mother if everyone around you is negative. It's hard to build a life of greatness for your child, if everyone around you is content with mediocrity. So, take a moment, think about the top five people who you call on regularly for friendship and really think about the kind of energy they give out. Are they shining light into your life? Or are they more often consumed with darkness. If you want to change your situations, you have to check your village, and adjust as necessary.

The business of co-parenting requires what I like to call

The 5 C's of Co-Parenting:

1) Communication;

2) Compromise;

3) Conflict Prevention;

4) Consideration; and

5) Cooperation.

❖ *Communication*

Communication is one of the most important aspects of ANY relationship. But it is especially important when co-parenting. Even if you believe that certain things are common sense and you should not have to *literally* communicate those things, it is in the best interest of all parties involved that you clearly communicate your thoughts whenever possible. No two people think alike. For example, just because it makes sense to me that my four-year-old should not be allowed to play outside around the neighborhood without adult supervision, does not mean that others believe the same. In fact, I have a neighbor whose two and three-year-old children run all around the neighborhood by themselves. Again, just because it makes sense to *me* that smoking in the presence of your children is not only inappropriate, but also a health risk, I have met people who smoke around their children on a daily basis and do not give it a second thought.

The point is, it is not reasonable to assume that others think and do exactly as you. Nor can you always expect people to know your expectations. Most of us cannot read minds (although some claim to have this power). If you want someone to know something, you have to communicate that something - even if you believe they should know without you telling them. It is better to communicate too much (effectively) than too little. Now, the subject of how to effectively communicate is literally a completely independent topic for another book. However, here are some very basic tips to keep in mind when communicating with your child's mother:

1) <u>Remain cool, calm, collected, and respectful</u> - Keep your emotions out of it. If you are angry, upset, frustrated, or just annoyed with her, try to wait until you have cooled off. Once you have cooled off, think of a tactful way to communicate

your position to her. Talk *to* her, not *down* to her. Having a condescending tone will only make matters worse. Regardless of how you feel, disrespect is a no-no. No yelling, no profanity allowed. A good approach is to follow the motto "If you don't have anything nice to say, don't say anything at all." While it's okay and oftentimes necessary to explain your position, whether it be agreement or disagreement, you must always do so respectfully.

2) <u>Be clear</u> - Say what you mean, mean what you say. As previously mentioned, most of us aren't mind readers. Never assume that your child's mother "knows" what you want or need from her and that you are on the same page. You need to be clear in your expectations and make sure that she understands them.

3) <u>Communicate in writing as much as possible</u> - When it comes to communication related to your child, it's best to communicate in writing as much as possible. If you have an important conversation, send a follow up email to confirm the conversation to ensure you are in agreement. Not only does this avoid confusion about what exactly was said, but it

also creates a record for you to use in the future if necessary. However, when communicating in writing, try to be mindful of your tone and your choice of words, as unlike verbal communication, you can't take back a text message or email that has been sent.

❖ *Compromise*

The bottom line is both parents cannot always get what they want when it comes to decisions concerning their child. Therefore, while you may *know* what's best, please remember there are two of you, both parents, whose opinions matter. The best way to prevent potential problems due to disagreement is to understand the importance of compromise. Pick your battles - everything is not worth the fight. Before making a fuss about an issue, make sure that you have had ample opportunity to clearly view the full picture. You have to decide what's important to fight over, and what you are willing to compromise on. Carefully consider your child's mother's position. Does any of it make sense? Will going with her suggestion hurt your situation? Or are you simply disagreeing because it's not what you had in mind? Insisting that things always go your way, specifically without being reasonable, is not co-parenting and will likely lead to more stress and chaos in the long run.

❖ *Conflict Prevention*

I cannot stress enough the importance of being proactive. Discuss issues that may come up later such as religion, education, traveling out of the country, holidays, vacation, when and how to introduce your child to someone you are seriously dating, who is allowed to babysit your child, etc. It's important that you and your child's mother establish as many agreements as possible regarding your child while the two of you are on good terms. As mentioned previously, it's even more important that you formalize your agreements and obtain court orders. Another good idea is to put a system in place that will prevent deadlock such as "rock, paper, scissors," drawing out of a hat, flipping a coin, or asking a third, neutral party to make the final decision in the event that you are unable to agree on an issue. This may sound trivial now, but believe me, it may solve problems that are far from trivial when in the heat of the moment.

❖ *Consideration*

Because there are two parents and one child (or several children), it's important to always have consideration for each other. You must be considerate of each other's time, schedule, feelings, and relationship with your child. Before making major decisions related to your child, discuss them with your child's mother so that she can give her input. Before making plans with your child that may interfere with your child's mother's custodial time, discuss your proposed plans with her and a possible way to make up that missed time if she wants. Be considerate of her feelings. Unless the two of you just have a close, friendly relationship, do not discuss your personal affairs with your child's mother. Discussions about whom you are dating and your love life (outside of that which is relevant to your child) could possibly cause jealousy, or other ill feelings from your child's mother and will result in unnecessary tension in your co-parenting relationship.

Always remain considerate of your child's relationship with his or her mother. Encourage your child to continue to develop the bond with their mother. In spite of how you feel about your child's mother, do not say or do things that will make your child uncomfortable about having a relationship with his or her mother. Do not make or allow others to make any negative comments to or within the hearing distance of your child, no matter how true they may be. If your child's mom is a deadbeat, it's unnecessary for you to remind your child of this. If your child's mother isn't parenting up to your standards, that's not your child's business; that is between you and your child's mother. Most importantly, do not argue with your child's mother in front of your child. Your disagreements are private matters to be discussed between the two of you. The last thing you need is for your child to develop ill feelings for you or his or her mother due to your comments and actions. This may be very hard to do, but it is crucially important. Always be the bigger person. Trust me, your child will learn what he or she needs to learn about their mother on their own, without any input from you. It's better that they learn on their own so that they do not have bitterness towards you in the future.

❖ Cooperation

Co-parenting is all about teamwork. The business of co-parenting will be considerably more successful if you and your child's mother support one another. This means that the two of you should attempt to, at a minimum, have similar parenting ideals and make sure that your child understands that you are working together for their benefit. If you have an issue with your child, make an effort to incorporate your child's mother into your discipline method, even if that just means making a phone call to her in front of your child and informing her about the problem. If for one reason or another your child's mother cannot keep her scheduled visitation, help out if you are able to; switch days with her, keep your child an extra day or two, and depend on her to do the same for you.

When it comes to your child's education and extracurricular activities, make sure that you and your child's mother are involved as much as possible. Attend parent-teacher conferences and parent council meetings together. When you send correspondence to your child's school, make sure that both of your names are signed on the correspondence whenever practical so that the school is aware that both parents are involved. Cheer your child on together at events. It may seem awkward at first, but you'll get used to it and it will put your child at ease. Remember at the beginning of this book when I said I have personal experience? Trust me, I do. My husband and I have attended numerous parent-teacher conferences with my stepson's mother and most recently, his step-father has also attended. As a result, the teacher and other administrators at his school recognized that my stepson has a strong support system. We also attend sports events, award assemblies, and occasionally even birthday parties for my stepson together. Even if we don't sit together the entire time, we acknowledge one another, and interact peacefully. From the outside looking in, you are not able to tell that any ill feelings ever existed between our two homes, and believe me, at one point there was some extreme illness happening. While initially all of this may have been a bit awkward, ultimately, the benefits outweighed the awkwardness as our divided/blended family has progressed and, as a result, our family lives in peace.

I know the concept of the business of co-parenting may seem like a lot of work. Especially if you have to work hard in an effort to influence your child's mother to get on the same page, set aside the drama, and work with you in considering the best interests of your child. But, although it is a process that requires a lot of consideration, strategy, and action on your behalf, tackling the issues discussed in this book and taking action will ultimately pay off. Regardless of what your child's mother does or does not do, you and your child deserve to live in peace. This means that in order to achieve this peace, you have to step out of your comfort zone and take control as the parenting Partner of your divided family. Much of the success of your co-parenting relationship depends largely on you. Keep in mind that even the simplest decisions you make may detrimentally affect your child both now and later. The good news is, by making smart, selfless decisions now, your child has a greater chance of having a bright future. And that's the business of co-parenting.

MEET MERISSA V. GRAYSON

Also known as "America's Blended Family Expert," Merissa V. Grayson is a dynamic and driven Lawyer, Author, Mediator and Co-Parenting + Blended Family Advocate.

Merissa's background stems not only from her professional experience as a Child Custody & Family Law Attorney, but also from her experience as a Wife and Stepmother who has personally disentangled the difficult challenges that often come with the territory of divided & blended family living.

Merissa has dedicated her life to helping families around the country tackle similar challenges by truly walking them through positive transformations to help them gain the lifestyle and peace of mind they deserve.

Made in the USA
Charleston, SC
24 April 2016